THE
ELEMENTS
OF
MENTALITY

THE
ELEMENTS
OF
MENTALITY

*The Foundations of
Psychology and Philosophy*

DAVID HUME

ECW PRESS
ecwpress.com

To be published by ECW PRESS Fall 2003
2120 Queen Street East, Suite 200, Toronto, Ontario, Canada M4E 1E2

[CATALOGUING IN PUBLICATION DATA]

Hume, David
Elements of mentality : the foundations of psychology and philosophy / David Hume.

ISBN 1-55022-601-0

1. Psychology and philosophy. I. Title.

BF51.H86 2003   100   c2002-902028-2

Cover and Text Design: Daniel Crack, Kinetics Design
Production & Typesetting: Kinetics Design
Printing: Transcontinental

This book is set in Giovanni and Trajan

DISTRIBUTION
CANADA: Jaguar Book Group, 100 Armstrong Avenue, Georgetown, ON, L7G 5S4
USA: IPG 814 North Franklin Street, Chicago, IL 60610

PRINTED AND BOUND IN CANADA

ECW PRESS
ecwpress.com

There is no question of importance, whose decision is not comprised in the science of man; and there is none, which can be decided with any certainty, before we become acquainted with that science. In pretending, therefore, to explain the principles of human nature, we in effect propose a complete system of the sciences, built on a foundation almost entirely new, and the only one upon which they can stand with any certainty.

DAVID HUME, *A Treatise of Human Nature*, 1739

TABLE OF
CONTENTS

ANALYTICAL
TABLE OF
CONTENTS

PROLOGUE

B Y dictionary definition, "psychology" is the study of the psyche, the workings of the mind, mentality. By this definition, psychology is primarily the effort to understand subjective experience. Nothing seems more mundane and clear than the flow of subjective experiences that constitute normal life. But nothing has proven more elusive than a coherent articulation of the principles by which subjective life seems to make sense. Everyone is continuously trying to understand his experiences, and everyone is naturally curious about the principles involved, but the current state of psychology provides little satisfaction.

Walking also seems simple. One is able to walk without being able to articulate the principles that achieve that immensely complex athletic task. To walk, one has developed a perfectly good understanding of walking that allows one to walk competently without being able to articulate that understanding. One's understanding of walking is almost entirely tacit. Today, scientists are confident that the branch of physics called "classical mechanics" affords, if only in theory, a complete explanation of the physical aspects of walking, but there is no comparable set of principles by which subjective experiences can be understood, even in theory.

One has a tacit understanding of one's experiences that, for the most part, works as comfortably as one's understanding of walking. This book attempts to articulate the tacit understanding of the flow of one's experiences that one applies routinely without troubling to analyze or articulate that understanding. Just as classical physics provides a complete theoretical explanation of walking, one's tacit understanding can provide a complete theoretical explanation of one's experiences — at least that is the contention of this book. If so, the elusive goal of psychology — to understand the psyche — is attained by the articulation of that tacit understanding, and everyone's natural curiosity about his own experiences may be satisfied.

Once the organizing principles of mentality are laid bare, however, they offer more than a basis for understanding the flow of experiences that constitute ordinary life. They also offer a basis for understanding the entire structure of knowledge, including the most extraordinary and unusual issues. The structure of knowledge is the field of philosophy. There is an intimate connection between philosophy and psychology: ideas, of which knowledge is composed, are a type of experience, a psychological phenomenon. The principles according to which all experiences are organized could be called the philosophy of psychology, and the principles according to which ideas are structured could be called the psychology of philosophy: the organizing principles are the same for both disciplines. At the foundational level, psychology and philosophy merge. For psychology and philosophy, the significance of this book is the same: it articulates the common foundations of both.

This book consists of three parts which are, essentially, three essays. The first part, The Elemental Model of Mentality, identifies the different types of elemental experiences and describes the principles by which those experiences are organized. Together, the identification of the elements and the principles of their organization constitute the elemental model of mentality. The elemental model can serve as the foundation for any psychological analysis. In addition, the elemental model has implications about the nature of reality and the structure of knowledge. Those implications give rise to an entire philosophy (elementalism) of which the basic principles are described in the second part, The Philosophy of Elementalism. The third part, Elementalism and the Mind/Matter Problem, applies those principles to a set of long-standing philosophical issues that fall under the general name of the mind/matter (or mind/brain or mind/body) problem. Whereas everyone is naturally interested in understanding his ordinary experiences, philosophical mind/matter issues interest a smaller group. However, within philosophical circles, the mind/matter problem is significant, and the philosophy of elementalism offers a solution.

PART ONE

THE
ELEMENTAL
MODEL
OF
MENTALITY

INTRODUCTION

T
O understand the operation of a car, one develops a conceptual model that consists of both the identification of the functionally significant parts of the car and a description of the basic function of each of those parts. For example, the particular parts that one's conceptual model of a car must identify include the steering wheel, the accelerator pedal, and the brake pedal. To describe the basic function of the steering wheel one might say, "When the car is moving forward, clockwise rotation of the steering wheel turns the car to the right; counter-clockwise rotation turns it to the left." To steer the car one need know nothing about the mechanics of the steering system, which may be complicated beyond comprehension, provided that one understands the basic function of the steering wheel. Furthermore, the description of the basic function of a steering wheel is true for all cars, even though no two cars have identical steering characteristics.

In the process of intellectual development, one creates a conceptual model of one's mentality that also identifies parts and describes their functions. In that model, the "parts," or elements, are types of mental experiences. This part of this book describes a model of mentality by identifying the different types of mental experiences and by describing their basic functions with some precision. The elements are identified by common English terms, which reflect a core of common understanding.

On the other hand, the synthesis of the model from the elements has not previously been articulated. Fortuitously, the model composed from elemental experiences seems complete, and there is no need to hypothesize the involvement of unexperienced factors (such as a subconscious) to explain any aspect of subjective life or behavior.

There is a fundamental difference between the "parts" that constitute one's model of a car and the types of mental experiences that make up one's model of mentality. On the one hand, automobile parts always consist of more elementary constituents, and there is no reason to suppose that the entities known today as elementary physical particles are not themselves constituted from more elementary constituents ad infinitum. On the other hand, the mental experiences identified in this part of this book are genuinely elemental in the sense that they are incapable of analysis into more elementary constituents.

By the term "basic functions," I intend to describe the functions of elemental experiences only in normal circumstances. Although a steering system may malfunction in countless ways or may, for example, affect the flight path of a car that is driven at high speed over a cliff, those circumstances are not normal for the operation of a car. The description of the basic function of the steering wheel might be incorrect in some unusual circumstances. Similarly, I intend the description offered below of the functions of mental experiences to apply only in the state of full waking consciousness of one who is mentally competent.

Chapter One describes the various types of mental experiences along with the basic function of each type. Chapter Two explains how the basic functions interrelate within an overall process of "mentation." Mentation is the sequential organization of elemental mental experiences that defines, and deals with, reality. Together, Chapters One and Two describe a model of mentality that can serve to analyze any psychological phenomena. But the description that appears in these first two chapters is not proof that the model is true. Considerations such as proof and truth lead us to Chapter Three, which deals with the philosophy of elementalism that emerges from the model and that can serve as the foundation for analysis of any philosophical issue.

CHAPTER ONE

THE
ELEMENTS

J UST as the elements of physics are types of physical entities (e.g., quarks, strings), the elements of mentality are types of mental experiences. In any model, an entity is only an element (therefore, elemental) if it is incapable of analysis (reduction) into more elementary constituents. There are five distinct families of elemental mental experiences:

- external sensory experiences
- internal bodily experiences
- emotional experiences
- intellectual experiences (called "concepts" or "ideas")
- experiences of the will (called "concentrational experiences" or "concentrations")

The taxonomy of mental experiences into these distinct types is exhaustive. There are no other types of experiences, no intermediate categories, no hybrids. Nor is subjective life constituted of anything other than these types of experiences. This chapter describes these five families of mental experiences.

To identify the different types of experiences serves to distinguish one type from another, for example, to distinguish a visual experience from an idea

*and from an emotion. A less obvious difficulty is to distinguish one experi-
ence from another of the same type, particularly from its immediate
predecessor or successor of the same type. Where does one sound end and
the next begin? This issue is addressed in The Unit of Mentation in
Chapter Two, Mentation.*

Consider the first three families of experiences (external sensory experiences, internal bodily experiences, and emotions). When one experiences
a tactile experience, one is said to "feel" it. One also feels one's balance,
and one feels rhythm. One feels hungry or sexually aroused or fatigued,
and one feels shame or joy. On the other hand, visual experiences are
seen, auditory experiences are heard, gustatory experiences are tasted,
and olfactory experiences are smelled. In common usage, the general
term "feel" may properly refer to any external sensory experience,
internal bodily experience, or emotion, unless there is a more specific
term (such as "see," "smell," and so on) that refers to that specific category of experience. Any experience that is felt is called a "feeling." Even
though visual or auditory experiences are not normally called "feelings,"
I use the term "feelings" to include any experience within these three
families of experiences because they all share a common characteristic:
value. Any external sensory, internal bodily, or emotional experience
has, as an inherent characteristic, the property of value. The other two
types of experiences (intellectual or concentrational experiences) do not
have the property of value.

Value is an inherent property of feelings. Value has no separate existence apart from being a property of the experiences of feelings, but this
form of existence includes everything that one considers to be valuable.

Value itself has two properties: first, value is either good (pleasing) or bad
(displeasing), and second, the goodness or badness of any particular
experience of a feeling has a magnitude (synonymous with intensity).
The goodness or badness of a feeling is an inherent property of that
feeling. The value of a feeling is experienced as part of the experience of
the feeling. Value is not a separate experience. Each experience of a
feeling is either good or bad, but not both. A complex circumstance

with good and bad aspects involves simultaneous separate feelings that include those different values. The magnitude of the value of a specific elemental experience lies somewhere on a spectrum from negligible to maximum magnitude. The magnitude of the value of the experience of a feeling is to be distinguished from the intensity of the experience itself. The intensity of the experience of a feeling refers to the strength or power with which the feeling is experienced. For example, the intensity of an auditory experience, a sound, is called its "volume." The intensity of a feeling may lie anywhere along a continuous spectrum from negligible to maximum intensity. The intensity of a feeling is related to, but is distinct from, the magnitude of the value of the experience (the volume of a sound is related to but distinct from the amount of pleasure or displeasure inherent in the experience of the sound).

There is a very simple relationship between emotions and value. First, each emotion is specifically good or bad. For example, every experience of shame always has bad value, and every experience of humor always has good value. Second, the magnitude of the value of an emotional experience is proportional to the intensity of the experience. For example, an experience of the emotion of fear at low intensity is called "anxiety" and the value of low-intensity fear is bad, but only mildly bad, i.e., badness of low magnitude. The experience of high-intensity fear is called "terror," and its value is extremely bad, i.e., badness of high magnitude.

For feelings other than emotions (external sensory and internal bodily experiences), the relationship between specific types of feelings and value is not simple. For example, one enjoys the coldness of ice cream in the summer but not necessarily in winter, and even when one does enjoy the coldness of ice cream, there is an optimum coldness beyond which colder is not better. There may be a simple formula that describes the relationship between the intensity of an external sensory or internal bodily experience and its value, but I have not discerned it. Instead of a simple formula, one's understanding of the relation between value and non-emotional feelings seems to consist of a catalogue of numerous very specific non-emotional feelings and the values that one has learned to expect in specific circumstances.

Even experiences of feelings with negligible value may have very important informational content. For example, the sound of a voice may or may not be pleasing like the sound of a musical note, but one may identify important information in the auditory experience of a voice. That information is intellectual content (see below in this chapter, Intellectual Experiences), and intellectual information is "important" to the extent that it portends value in the future — value that one can experience only as the property of future experiences of feelings.

There is a universal language of feelings (see below in this chapter, Instinctive Outputs and Instinctive Behavior) that consists of specific instinctive behaviors. This language includes such behaviors as tones of voice, facial expressions, postures, and so on. These specific behaviors are caused by specific feelings, but not every experience of every feeling has a specific, unambiguous behavior associated with it. I offer no formula describing which feelings give rise to which behaviors except that the instinctive behaviors seem directly related to value. An experience of significant value will be reflected in some type of instinctive behavior. On the other hand, sounds or sights with only informational value do not seem to give rise to instinctive expressions.

> One interprets the instinctive behavior of others as a communication of how they feel. What one understands as a communication, by whatever means, contains only intellectual, not emotional or other, content or value — i.e., what one understands as a communication of another person's emotional experience is one's own present concept that the other person experiences a particular emotion, and that concept is an intellectual experience of one's own that may or may not give rise to one's own emotional experiences.

Value, which exists only as a property of feelings, provides what is called "purpose" or "meaning" to life and is the sole currency by which the economics of all decisions and exchanges are measured. (See Chapters Two and Three, below.)

EXTERNAL SENSORY EXPERIENCES

External sensory experiences are the feelings that one interprets as resulting from direct communication with the external physical world. These experiences include the experiences that correspond to the common description of the five external senses, i.e., the visual, tactile, auditory, olfactory, and gustatory senses, but there are two additional categories of external sensory experiences: the feeling that one identifies with being accelerated (including rotated) and gives rise to one's "sense of balance" (hereinafter called an "acceleratory" experience), and the feeling that one identifies with the passage of time and gives rise to one's "sense of rhythm" (hereinafter called a "rhythmic" experience, although reference to a cyclical or percussive character is not intended). External sensory experiences serve to define, and to locate one within, time and space. The totality of one's external sensory experiences is interpreted by the intellect, and that interpretation is one's understanding of external reality.

All visual experiences have visual characteristics (whatever characteristics make the experiences visual: a visual field with areas of color and brightness, binocular "depth," and so on), but each visual experience has its own arrangement of those characteristics. The unique arrangement of the visual characteristics of a visual experience (the characteristics that distinguish one visual experience from another) forms its "content." The content of a visual experience must be distinguished from what the experience seems to represent. For example, consider a visual experience that one interprets as one's face in a mirror. The content of the visual experience consists of the arrangement of colors and intensities at different areas of the visual field. The idea that this arrangement of visual characteristics represents, for example, a face is not part of the visual experience. Rather, the idea is a separate experience, an intellectual experience or concept (see below, Intellectual Experiences). Together, particular external sensory experiences and the concept that they represent something specific constitute what is called a "perception." Thus, a perception is not elemental. Rather, it is a composite of elements.

INTERNAL BODILY EXPERIENCES

These are the feelings that one identifies with a particular internal bodily location caused not by direct communication with the external world but by some internal bodily function, for example, proprioception, muscle fatigue, hunger, lack of oxygen, sexual arousal, drowsiness, and so on. The bodily functions themselves are not the internal bodily experiences. Rather, the experiences are the feelings that one comes to understand are caused by the bodily functions. A complete list of internal bodily experiences would include not only the experiences relating to every perceptible normal bodily cycle but also those of every possible malfunction or disease.

EMOTIONS

An emotion is an intellectually caused feeling. Each emotional experience is caused by concentration on a particular intellectual concept. (For "concentration," see below, in this chapter, Will). An emotional experience has four aspects:

- the particular intellectual concept giving rise to the emotion
- the particular feeling that one identifies as the emotion (the feeling has value and intensity)
- a desire to behave according to a particular strategy with respect to the intellectual concept giving rise to the emotion
- a particular bodily change exactly appropriate to the behavior desired

For example, one sees a lion and (1) conceives a present danger; that concept of danger evokes fear, an emotion that includes (2) the feeling identified as fear and (3) the desire to flee the danger (strategic behavioral desire), all of which are accompanied by (4) physiological bodily changes (experienced as internal bodily experiences) appropriate to sprinting. One experiences the four aspects simultaneously as a single composite, so that (1) the seriousness of the conceived danger translates directly into (2) the intensity of the feeling and value, into (3) the intensity of the desire to implement the strategy of sprinting away from the danger, and into (4) the magnitude of the bodily change. But one is not compelled to run and may decide to do nothing or even to attack, based on other aspects of the present circumstances.

Emotions have the following additional characteristics.

First, each emotion is associated with another specific emotion, which is its negative or opposite: one of the pair is good, and the other, bad. Opposite emotions cannot be experienced simultaneously. Furthermore, a trauma (or religious experience) to one emotion causes damage to the opposite emotion. Both of these factors suggest that each pair of emotions is the result of one physiological system. Any number of non-opposite emotions may be experienced simultaneously. Some combinations of emotions commonly experienced simultaneously are identified below by the name given to the combination — for instance, jealousy is the combination of esteem and resentment. While individual emotions are elemental constants, a combination of emotions may differ with each experience, because the relative intensities of the individual emotions may differ and because there may be other emotions experienced simultaneously.

Second, sustained, low-intensity emotional experiences are called "moods." There seems to be a maximum intensity threshold beyond which the character of an emotional experience changes as though its circuits were overloaded. Such overloading damages the emotional machinery, whether like a small scar or like a completely immobilizing fracture. Overloading of a bad emotion is called a "traumatic" experience, and overloading of a good emotion is called a "religious" or "spiritual" experience, an "epiphany." Similarly, there appears also to be a duration threshold, as with extended and continuous sorrow, shame, or despair of even minor intensity, beyond which the machinery of that emotion can be permanently affected. What I intend by the term "basic function" of experiences does not apply when these thresholds are exceeded.

Third, the inherent desire associated with each emotion is both strategic (or generic) and behavioral. It is strategic because the desire contains no specifics as to how to implement the strategy (the specifics are intellectually determined). It is behavioral because implementation of the strategy usually involves a characteristic behavior appropriate to the emotional bodily change (for example, flight from danger characteristically involves sprinting). The strategic behavioral desires that are inherent aspects of emotions are the only behavioral directions that one experiences.

Feelings other than emotions (i.e., sensory and bodily experiences) provide value in the present but offer no direction as to behavior in the future, nor do the other two types of mental experiences (concepts and concentrations). Emotions, with their generic behavioral desires, are the only experiences constituting motivation. There is no such thing as an elemental "need" in the sense that the need itself motivates one to satisfy the need. One experiences not needs but only feelings; for example, one needs nutrition, but one may feel hungry when not in need of nutrition, and one may be in need of nutrition yet not feel hungry. In each case, one's behavior relates to the feeling that one experiences (the hunger), not to the need. One may conceive that the need is the physiological cause of the feeling, but the conception is an intellectual experience, and the need is not itself experienced.

Fourth, one cannot directly turn an emotion on or off simply by deciding to do so. Decisions, however, can somewhat control emotions indirectly by affecting concentration. For example, one can overcome one's fear of the lion by concentrating on one's ability to kill it so that it represents not a present danger but a challenge. Only in this indirect sense can decisions affect emotions. (See Chapter Two.)

The Eleven Pairs of Emotions
This section describes the eleven pairs of emotions. Frequently, there are words that describe the same emotion at different intensities. For instance, annoyance, anger, and rage are different intensities of the same emotion. In the description that follows, anger will include both annoyance and rage.

PAIRS OF EMOTIONS

Good	Bad
Pride	*Shame*
Esteem	*Contempt*
Gutsiness	*Fear*
Humor	*Anger*
Love	*Hatred*
Attraction	*Revulsion*
Joy	*Sorrow*
Gratitude	*Greed*
Pity	*Resentment*
Curiosity	*Boredom*
Hope	*Despair*

Pride and Shame. The intellectual concept giving rise to pride is personal accomplishment or success: the successful outcome of an attempt to achieve a goal. The strategic behavioral desire associated with pride is the desire to communicate the fact of the accomplishment to others — to share the success. The intellectual concept that gives rise to shame is personal failure (the unsuccessful outcome of an attempt to achieve a goal), and it is felt as a desire to withdraw to privacy so as to keep the failure secret — to hide in shame. Shame is called "embarrassment" when one is unable to keep the failure secret and perceives others as recognizing the failure. One experiencing shame but behaving in a forthright manner about the failure is said to have honor. (See Acting, in Chapter Two.)

When the personal failure causes harm to another, the resulting shame is called "guilt" and is the basis of what is called one's "conscience." An act constituting a personal failure and intentionally (*mens rea*) causing harm to another is called "immoral" or "criminal." Shame is the simple elemental basis for the human capacity to make distinctions concerning right and wrong — i.e., morality or ethics. Most moral debates concern the standards by which actions are to be judged a failure or not. Appropriate standards differ with social circumstances, to say nothing of different evolutionary stages. Those standards are intellectual determinations and vary, but at all times and places the capacity to make distinctions between right and wrong is the same: the elemental basis of morality (the emotion of shame) is a universal human constant.

Esteem and Contempt. Whereas one's own success gives rise to pride, another person's success in achieving one's own goals gives rise to esteem. Similarly, another person's failure to achieve one's goals gives rise to contempt. Esteem is experienced as a desire to praise (to honor), and contempt, to ridicule (to place shame upon).

Fear and Gutsiness. The concept that evokes fear is present danger — i.e., the probability of imminent bad experiences. Fear is felt as a desire to flee in order to avoid the probable badness. "Gutsiness" is a slang term. Gutsiness is caused by the concept of a challenge — i.e., a probability of overcoming the risk of danger with effort. Gutsiness manifests itself as a desire to take on the challenge and is distinct from any element of wanting to do harm, as in resentment or hatred. Fear ranges from anxiety, at low intensity, through fear at moderate intensity, to terror at high intensity. Gutsiness at moderate intensity is called "confidence." A person experiencing fear but behaving gutsily and trying to call forth guts is said to have courage. One actually feeling gutsy needs no courage. One who yields to one's fear when one ought to be courageous is called a "coward." Arrogance is the combination of contempt and gutsiness.

Anger and Humor. Anger is caused by the concept that one is the victim of a disrespect — an intentional interference by the perpetrator with one's attempt to achieve a goal. Anger ranges from annoyance at low intensity, through anger, to rage at high intensity. Anger is felt as a desire to punish the perpetrator of the disrespect. The objective of the punishment is to "teach a lesson" that the disrespect was improper — that one's thwarted goal was legitimate.

Just as the underlying emotional foundation of morality is shame, so that of justice is anger. The justice of any particular situation depends on the appropriateness of the victim's goal or the meaning of intention or the appropriate punishment, but the elemental foundation of justice (the emotion of anger) is an inherent human constant.

An injustice may or may not also be an immorality. Where an injustice is not an immorality, the punishment is considered just where it exacts fair compensation and an apology. An apology is an acknowledgment by the perpetrator that he has learned the lesson of the impropriety of the disrespect — a demonstration of shame for failing to maintain the proper standard of civility. Where the injustice is also an immorality, in addition to anger, the emotion of hatred is evoked, and then the punishment is considered just if there is retribution as well as compensation and an apology.

I have found no English word that precisely connotes the emotion opposite to anger. The word "humor" refers to things that are humorous rather than to the feeling one experiences when one enjoys humorous things. What is intended here is the feeling — the feeling that accompanies humorous laughter (perhaps "mirth"). One experiences humor when one conceives a disrespect that abruptly juxtaposes the victim prior to the disrespect with the victim after the disrespect, provided that one identifies with the perpetrator rather than with the victim, even if one is the victim (taking a joke). Humor is the enjoyment of causing the victim spontaneously to react to unexpected interference with his attempt to achieve a goal — the indignity of the victim's momentary confusion. There is no humor without a victim of a disrespect.

Love and Hatred. The concept that causes love is something that deserves and needs protection (often because of its beauty and/or vulnerability — its innocence). Love is felt as a desire to nurture and protect and is not necessarily part of "romantic love" or "falling in love." "To love" is also to be distinguished from "to like," which is often understood to mean "to love moderately." (See below, Attraction and Revulsion.) Liking and loving may go well together, but they are two separate emotions, and it is not uncommon for one to love, but to dislike, another. The term "affection" ambiguously includes both liking and loving.

The concept that evokes hatred is "evil" — i.e., the intention in another to cause one to experience harm (badness). Hatred is felt as a desire to eliminate the evil. Where the evil intention can be "cleansed," hatred manifests itself as a desire to eliminate the evil through retribution (exorcism). Where a serious evil has permeated a person and cannot be cleansed, however, hatred manifests itself as a desire to kill. Killing is the appropriate strategy towards an incorrigible enemy for whom one has no use and without whom, one imagines, the world would be better off.

Attraction and Revulsion (Liking and Disliking). The concepts that cause these emotions are matters of preference and taste. One has the capacity to develop tastes where one has a choice. The concept that gives rise to attraction is a choice of objects that one might possess that differ in some respect, and it is the differences that one finds attractive or repulsive. Individuals' tastes differ and may change over time. This does not imply that individuals are free to change their tastes at will. In some cases, one seems to discover the taste within oneself once and for all (sexual orientation). In other areas, one never seems finally at home (clothing). How tastes are formed, and how and to what extent they are changeable thereafter, are unpredictable matters of whimsy and caprice. Nor is there any apparent organizing principle that explains what people like or dislike.

Attraction manifests itself as a desire to take possession of the object that is desired or liked. "Possession" in this sense does not mean "legal ownership to the exclusion of others." Rather, it means "having available for experiencing at one's will." Thus one who likes skiing will want to ski as long as one likes it. One who likes another person will want to have that other person available in order to experience whatever it is about that other that one likes. There is no element of exclusivity of possession with attraction: exclusivity is an aspect of such emotions as greed or resentment.

What gives rise to revulsion is also a matter of taste, but the behavioral desire associated with revulsion is always the same, and that is to avoid the disliked object — to dispossess or disown it. Intense revulsion is called "horror."

Joy and Sorrow. Whereas attraction manifests itself as a desire to take possession, joy is the emotion experienced when one actually gains possession of the desired object. Joy manifests itself as a desire to celebrate — to play. Play is any activity that is fun. Having fun is synonymous with experiencing joy. Extreme joy is called "bliss" or "exhilaration." "Happiness" refers to a mythical blissful state of mind in which all experiences are good and none are bad. There is no such state, but there is joy. I am unable descriptively to characterize the activities that constitute play except to note that they can be utterly frivolous and otherwise purposeless.

Sorrow is the feeling experienced upon losing something previously possessed. Sorrow is the experience of loss. Intense sorrow is called "grief." Sorrow manifests as a desire to grieve.

Gratitude and Greed. The concept that evokes gratitude is the receipt from a benefactor of something earned — earned in the sense that the recipient has paid for it in the only currency of value (feelings), whether or not payment was made to the benefactor. Gratitude manifests itself as a desire to express gratitude to the benefactor. Piety and humility are expressions of gratitude. Relief is gratitude.

The concept that causes greed is the opportunity to receive something unearned — "something for nothing." Greed manifests itself as a desire to take advantage of the opportunity and to derive benefit that one has not earned. Laziness and gossip are expressions of greed.

Pity and Resentment. The concept that causes resentment is another's undeserved goodness, particularly (but not exclusively) if it results from the implementation of that other's greed. Resentment manifests itself as a desire to bring that person to experience comparable badness. Jealousy is the apparently contradictory combination of resentment and esteem.

The intellectual concept that gives rise to pity is another's undeserved bad experiences. Pity manifests itself as a desire to help.

Curiosity and Boredom. "Mystery that is solvable with exploratory effort" is the concept that causes curiosity, and curiosity is felt as a desire to explore in order to find a solution. Interest is synonymous with curiosity. The principal emotional element of surprise, confusion, awe, and wonder is interest.

The intellectual concept giving rise to boredom is a circumstance that is fully understood in the sense that further exploration will not yield greater understanding. Boredom manifests itself as a desire to be occupied with anything else.

"An interesting job" is the definition of occupational success. A life of boredom is called "misery."

Hope and Despair. The concept that causes hope is the "possibility of success, if one makes the proper effort, despite the risk of failure." Hope manifests itself as a desire to make whatever effort is necessary to achieve the favorable outcome, including hoping. Hoping is an attempt to invoke magic or luck by the use of will power (see below, Will). In the case of physically diseased individuals, the physiological changes associated with hope sometimes do appear to achieve magic. Acting hopeful in the face of highly probable failure is called "heroism."

The concept giving rise to despair is the probability of failure no matter what effort one exerts. Despair manifests itself as a desire to do nothing and, ultimately, to die. Sustained or severe despair is called "depression."

The above list constitutes a complete catalogue of the twenty-two human emotions. A normal mental structure has the full capability for each emotion, including its invocation by concentration on a specific intellectual concept, its specific feeling, its strategic behavioral desire, and its bodily change. Extreme examples of abnormal emotional structure would include the lack of an emotion altogether or the constant experience of a particular emotion — for example, the lack of guilt or pity, the constant experience of fear or despair. No doubt there can be mental disorders within a normal emotional structure, but any structural abnormality will result in strange behavior.

INTELLECTUAL EXPERIENCES (CONCEPTS OR IDEAS)

Intellectual experiences are the experiences of concepts (synonymous with ideas). Concepts are the only intellectual types of experiences. One does not experience a concept except as a solution to a problem posed to the intellect in the context of mentation (see Chapter Two, Mentation).

The content of a concept does not self-generate from nothing. One does not conceive of multiplication without first conceiving addition. One does not conceive of any aspect of external physical reality without first experiencing external sensory experiences, which are the basis of one's concept of external physical reality. Similarly, every concept derives from other experiences. The content of a concept includes a relationship between other experiences. I call those other experiences "original" with respect to the concept that relates them.

The number "one half" illustrates that the content of a concept is a relation between other experiences. The concept of the number "one" and the concept of the number "two" are separate concepts, and the concept "one half" is also a separate concept in its own right, the content of which is a relationship between the concepts "one" and "two," which are the original experiences related by the concept "one half." The concept "one half" contains nothing other than that relationship between the concept "one" and the concept "two," and yet the concept "one half" is as much a separate concept as the concepts "one" or "two," and it can serve as an original experience for other numbers just as one and two serve as original experiences for one half. Furthermore, just as the concept "one half" derives from, and contains reference to, the concepts "one" and "two," those concepts themselves derive from their own original experiences.

A concept involves a relationship that the intellect has creatively drawn between other specific experiences (including other concepts). The principles on which the intellect draws conceptual relationships are known as "logic," "reason," or "sense." Logic is the set of principles by which the intellect is capable of creating concepts from other experiences. When it is experienced, every concept seems to make sense — that "seeming to make sense" is a part of the experience of the concept. A concept makes sense whether or not one can articulate the principles according to which it makes sense. That it seems to make sense is the property, or quality, or aspect of an experience that I call its "logicalness," or "logicality." One does not experience the logic by which a concept is created. Rather, one only experiences its bald logicality as part of the content of the concept — it seems to make sense. Unlike feelings, intellectual experiences do not have the qualities of value or intensity.

Just as color is a property of visual experiences, logicality is a property of intellectual experiences. Because logicality exists only as a property of an elemental experience, it cannot be defined in words. For example, the principles of the logic of hierarchies are described below, but those principles do not define the logicality of hierarchies. The statement of principles refers to a concept, in the experience of which the reader is invited to identify compelling hierarchical logicality. The statement of principles does not embody compelling intellectual authority (proof) — that authority exists only in the form of the logicality that one experiences as a property of the concept of those principles if they make sense.

Just as, for example, every visual experience has content that includes such visual qualities as the color and the brightness of particular areas of the visual field, each concept has intellectual content. The content of every intellectual experience includes four intellectual qualities:

- the problem that the concept was created to solve
- the original experiences that are related by the concept

- the relationship between the original experiences (one identifies this relationship as the concept, and this relationship is what one primarily remembers)
- the logicality of the relationship

There seem to be many exquisitely specialized logics applied by the intellect in particular situations. Taken together, they comprise the one grand logic by which one recognizes the sense (the common sense, or logic, or reasonableness) of all relationships that make sense. Logic, in all its aspects, is an inherent property of the intellect. Reasoning is the application of logic and is one's only means to achieve understanding or to choose behavior. The logical principles that inhere in one's intellect seem to be enduring, universal, and beneficently effective in the quest for value.

Intellectual Capabilities
Reasoning. Reasoning is the process that creates concepts, or solves problems, or applies logic — these three expressions are synonymous.

One can apply logic in two ways: by deduction, which is the recognition that certain experiences are related according to a particular logic, and by inference, which is the recognition of the logic or basis of the relationship between particular related experiences.

The process of reasoning is not experienced. Once a problem is posed, one experiences what one presumes is the result of a reasoning process only at the conclusion of the process, when one experiences the solution to the problem in the form of a newly created concept — a creation of the intellect. The new concept emerges complete (pops into consciousness), like the appearance of an image on a computer monitor. One does not experience partially created concepts that might reflect the process by which concepts are created any more than the images on a computer monitor reveal anything about the flow of dots and dashes within the central processing unit of a computer. One has no experience of how the reasoning process takes place or even that it is a process. A description of reasoning (as, for example, in a logic text) includes a sequence of concepts that lead logically from problem to solution but does not describe the reasoning process by which the author conceived each concept in the sequence or how the reader might determine whether or not each concept in the sequence makes sense. Only the logicality of the reader's intellectual experiences contains the "sense," the compelling intellectual authority.

Since one does not experience the conceptualizing process, and since there are numerous logics that could be logically applied in most circumstances, one cannot consistently predict what concept the intellect will create in any particular circumstance. The whole conceptual process, though perfectly logical in retrospect, seems magically creative in prospect. The conceptual process is at once logical yet unpredictable — indeterminate.

The ability to solve problems (to reason) does not include any ability to pose problems — to identify which problems should be solved, if any. The naked, problem-solving capability of the intellect does not include any self-directed volition that poses or identifies problems to solve. Chapter Two shows that problems are posed to the intellect, in the context of mentation, by the value of feelings and by strategic emotional desires.

Knowledge. The knowledge capability acquires, stores, and retrieves concepts. These functions, which do not include reasoning, constitute "cognition" within the narrowest meaning of that term.

Units of knowledge are concepts that are stored retrievably. One experiences the knowledge capability of the intellect only as and when knowledge is retrieved — i.e., only when a preconceived concept is experienced. One experiences not the retrieving process itself, but only its result, in the experience of the concept. Nor does one experience the acquisition or the storage processes. Acquisition of knowledge, the placing of concepts "in storage" in a retrievable form, seems to be an automatic consequence of every experience, even though the storage process may be very short-lived. Nor does one experience the loss of a memory as a separate experience.

The terms "acquisition," "storage," and "retrieval" suggest that there are processes of acquisition, of storage, of retrieval, but (as with reasoning) one does not experience any such processes, and there may be none. I use the terms only as metaphors by which the relationships between concepts can be understood.

The experience of a concept, when it is retrieved from storage, is undeniable, but its content may be incomplete or incorrect in comparison with the original as a consequence of cognitive imperfection.

The expression "on the tip of the tongue" represents a cognitive anomaly concerning retrieval of concepts that may seem to contradict the principle that concepts emerge complete, that one does not experience partial concepts. Remember that the content of an intellectual experience has four aspects: (1) the problem that the experience was created to solve, (2) the original experiences related by the concept, (3) the relationship between the original experiences, and (4) the logicality of the relationship. These four aspects are not equally important: the relationship between the original experiences (the third aspect) is far more important than the others. When a concept is recalled, most often it is the relationship between the original experiences that forms the recollection and the other three aspects may be forgotten. Even if all information of the other three aspects is forgotten, one still identifies the relationship between the original experiences as the concept. Of course, even that part, or parts of it, are often forgotten. Occasionally, as for instance when one is trying to remember a name, instead of experiencing the name, one experiences only a prodrome (or seeming premonition) of the name. When this happens, the name is said to be "on the tip of the tongue." One recognizes that the prodrome is not the name one was trying to remember, but rather, the prodrome contains some information of the other three aspects of the original experience of the name or some properties of the name, like some of the sounds or the number of syllables. When one recalls a name (or any other memory), the experience of the memory is an intellectual experience, a concept, whose content one recognizes as the solution to a particular problem. When one experiences a prodrome of a memory instead of the memory that one expected, the prodrome is also an intellectual experience whose content is (1) the properties of the intended memory that are included in the prodrome and (2) the concept that the prodrome is not the expected memory (not the complete solution to the current problem) but contains only some aspects of the expected concept. Thus, the prodrome is, itself, a concept that emerges complete even though it contains the content that it is merely part of the expected concept and may seem to be a partially experienced concept. Furthermore, the prodrome is a logical solution to the problem of recalling the name even though the prodrome is less complete than one had expected.

The prodrome purports to contain properties of the expected memory, but later when one actually recalls the memory, one learns that the properties contained in the prodrome may or may not be properties of the memory. But even if a prodrome accurately contains parts of the expected concept, the reasoning process remains concealed from experience. Curiously, the experience of a prodrome of a memory seems to block the fluent retrieval of the memory for some period of time.

Composite Concepts

The content of a concept embodies a logical relation between other experiences — for example, a logical relation between a visual and an auditory experience. The term "original experiences," in relation to a concept, refers to the experiences related by that concept. Since concepts are themselves experiences, a concept may embody the logical relation between, for example, a visual experience and a previous conceptual experience or between two previous conceptual experiences. The simplest concepts are those whose original experiences are not concepts but are individual sensory experiences. The term "initiating experiences" refers to original experiences that are non-conceptual. The term "composite concept" refers to a concept that relates other concepts — a concept whose original experiences are other concepts.

Somehow, the organization of knowledge facilitates the creation of composite concepts that logically relate separate concepts that were created previously but have no obvious relation to one another and may even seem contradictory. A composite concept is a type of synthesis of simpler concepts. It seems that any two concepts can be synthesized, even apparently contradictory concepts — for example, imaginary numbers. A composite concept can be an element of a concept yet more compositive, *ad infinitum*. For example, "laws of physics" is a separate concept drawn from (and analyzable into) numerous concepts that are themselves drawn from simpler concepts, and those from yet simpler ones, and so on, but only to the stage of initiating experiences, which cannot be further analyzed. Some of the types of composite concepts are memories, fantasies, and "abstract" or "pure" concepts, which are each described below.

As one experiences the first initiating experiences, one creates concepts to make sense of them by recognizing logical relations between them. Those concepts are experienced and, if they are not forgotten, stored to form the basis of composite concepts. Composite concepts may be synthesized into yet more composite concepts and so on, but ultimately all concepts derive from initiating experiences, not from concepts. In this way, knowledge is structured from non-conceptual experiences related logically (conceptually) to one another in hierarchical networks of concepts of increasing compositivity. Since a concept embodies a logical relationship between other experiences, the experience of a concept includes reference to those other experiences. Thus a composite concept can be analyzed (to the extent that memory allows) into the original concepts that it relates, and those into their original experiences, and so on, until the analysis reaches the stage of initiating experiences. In this way, knowledge can be analyzed, and its hierarchical structure revealed.

Knowledge is structured in hierarchical networks of concepts of increasing compositivity called "bodies of knowledge." In such a network, the elementary level consists of concepts whose original experiences are non-conceptual, and each succeeding level of increasing compositivity will include concepts that logically relate concepts at the prior level, until, at the most composite levels, a very few concepts relate all the prior levels. An example of such a body of knowledge would be the concept of "objective physical reality" — the "sciences." At the elementary level, the structure of the concept of objective reality consists of the huge number of individual concepts that relate one's individual external sensory experiences, whereas the top level contains the very few principles, called the "laws of physics," that are a logical synthesis containing, in principle, all those individual concepts. In theory, the laws of physics might reach the stage where they could predict the behavior of physical elements of which human bodies (including brains) are composed. At present, physics has not reached that degree of sophistication. and one understands other people by a different set of principles (a different body of knowledge) called "the humanities."

The elemental model of mentality suggests that one begins life equipped with a full complement of logics with which to conceptualize (to make sense of) experiences as they subsequently occur but that prior to initiating experiences one can experience no concepts (tabula rasa). The ideas of a full complement of intellectual capabilities and an initial tabula rasa of knowledge are not intended to imply that intellectual development actually occurs in this way. One may be born with some knowledge, as many animals seem to be, and logics may develop. This part of the book is not intended to address questions of developmental psychology. A different model may apply at early stages of intellectual development, but my conjecture is that the elemental model presented here begins to apply very early.

It may be impossible practically to analyze knowledge completely in terms of initiating experiences and simplest concepts. Consider the concepts of time and space — not the sophisticated mathematical understanding of a contemporary scientist, but the unarticulated working understanding of a young child. Even the child's understanding derives from countless external sensory experiences put together by the application of (presumably) numerous logics that the child has never articulated. Nor has anyone else. By the time one has acquired the language to attempt an analysis of the concept of time, one has long since forgotten the initiating experiences that led to the concept. Even apart from limitations of memory, the structure of the common working concept of time may be incomprehensibly complex (or perhaps incomprehensibly simple). Whatever the structure, one's composite concept of time is composed from simpler concepts whose initiating experiences include all of one's rhythmic experiences. The child's working understanding might seem primitive in comparison with a scientist's. In terms of compositivity, however, the scientist's might be only a marginal advance.

Five Basic Concepts and One Logic

The description of the types of elemental experiences and their functional properties constitutes a model by which all knowledge can, in principle, be analyzed into its most elementary, simple, fundamental (least composite) concepts, but this part does not actually perform that analysis. That effort is being made within such disciplines as developmental psychology and linguistics, within their separate areas. This part goes only so far as to describe the model, which is the basis on which the analysis occurs. Nor does this part of the book describe the numerous different logics. It is not at all clear to me how, or whether, a catalogue of logics might be developed in any systematic way.

Nevertheless, five concepts suggest themselves to me as minimally compositive:

- unity
- plurality
- order
- magnitude
- hierarchy

First, the concept of "individuality," or "unity," or "singularity," or "thing-ness" derives, initially, from a logic that allows one to identify a specific thing as distinct from everything else. This is to suggest not that there are "things" that are "distinct," but only that one's intellect contains a logic according to which one conceives of specific "things" as distinct from everything else. Second, after conceiving of a number of specific things, one then conceives (by means of a different logic) of the property those things have in common: thingness in general, unity in the abstract. The concept of unity is the basis of the mathematical concept of the number "1."

Second, "plurality" is the concept that refers to more than one thing. Plurality is the basis of the mathematical concept of a "set" of individual things.

Third, "order" refers to a particular arrangement of members of a set of things whereby one thing is next to a second, which may be next to a third, and so on, until the set is exhausted.

Fourth, "magnitude" is the property whereby one thing embodies more (or less or the same amount) of its own "thingness" (more or less of whatever the thing is) in comparison with a second thing.

Fifth, "hierarchy" is a set of things that are ordered in increasing (or decreasing) magnitude. The concept of hierarchy is the basis of the natural number system, which is a particular hierarchy, and the definition of a number is its position in that hierarchy.

The concept of hierarchy can serve to illustrate the particular logic of hierarchies. In the simplest hierarchy of increasing magnitude, each "thing" (each member of the hierarchy) has greater magnitude than the immediately preceding thing and less than its immediate successor — this is the definition of the simplest hierarchy of increasing magnitude. From this, the logic of hierarchies implies that each thing has greater magnitude than all its predecessors (not just the immediate one) and less magnitude than all its successors. For example, counting upwards from any number in the natural number system will not lead to a number that is less than the starting number, no matter how far one counts. How can one reach this implication without counting all the numbers? It is the inherent logic of hierarchies that allows one to draw this logical implication, without proof. One recognizes that the implication is logical by means of the logicality contained in the experience of the implication. Put another way, if A is greater than B, and B is greater than C, then it is the logic of hierarchies (and nothing else) that allows one to conclude that A is greater than C. The conclusion that A is greater than C seems intellectually compelling only to the extent that the experience of the concept of the conclusion includes hierarchical logicality.

Memories. The experience of a memory is not a re-experience of an earlier experience. Rather, it is the present experience of a concept with a particular type of content. The particular content of a concept that one identifies as a memory includes at least three elements: (1) a concept of one's physical and mental self, (2) a concept of hierarchical, progressive time, and (3) a concept that the particulars of the memory reflect an experience that one experienced in the past in its proper position after prior experiences and before subsequent experiences, to all of which it relates with logical continuity in all respects, not merely in its position in the temporal hierarchy. Merely because a concept purports to be a memory does not imply that it is correct as a reflection of the past. Rather, the logical continuity of one memory with all others gives credence to any particular memory.

As an intellectual experience, a memory has no "value" in itself. Unless the experience being recalled was itself an intellectual concept, the experience of a memory differs fundamentally from the original experience. For example, consider some kind of external sensory experience involving a physical pain. The memory of physical pain is not physically painful, because the memory is an intellectual experience without value, not an external sensory experience that does have value. The memory of emotional events may involve concepts similar to those that gave rise to the original emotions, and so the experience of the memory may give rise to newly felt emotions similar to the original experiences. But this may not always be the case. For example, what one once considered important may seem insignificant in retrospect.

Memory is fallible. Minor details of the content of a memory may be inaccurate or absent, even though in major respects the memory is accurate. Such unintended inaccuracies reflect imperfections in the knowledge capability of one's intellect.

Fantasies. Quite apart from unintended inaccuracies that reflect knowledge (cognitive) imperfection, the intellect also has the capability of purposefully retrieving memories outside the historical context in which they were created. When recalled, the stream of historically unrelated memories is called a fantasy. A memory is distinguishable from a fantasy only in that a memory is coherent with a huge network of other concepts that one identifies as memories whereas fantasies are isolated. But the entire network might be fantastic, and the isolated concept might be an accurate memory. A fantasy involving the memory of visual experiences is called a "dream" when it occurs in the sleeping state of consciousness. (States of consciousness are described below in this chapter, under Will.)

The ability to draw logical relationships between historically unrelated memories gives rise to fantasies. That ability is part of a more general ability to draw relationships between historically unrelated concepts in general, not merely memories. That general ability gives rise to "abstract concepts."

Abstract or Pure Concepts. Abstract concepts contain content about their relationships with other concepts but not about their prior history. For example, "1 + 1 = 2" is a concept that says nothing about the history of one's experiences of that concept but does relate the concepts "1," "+", "=", and "2", each of which derives from numerous other concepts, all of which are related in a great conceptual network that may seem silent concerning the history of one's experiences of those concepts. What is called "abstract reasoning" is a sequence of abstract concepts that are logically related to one another in that each is a logical step towards a solution (reached in the ultimate step in the sequence) of a problem (stated in the initial step). Simple problems can be solved in one step, but complex problems require a sequence of steps because of two intellectual limitations: first, there is a limit to the quantity of intellectual content that can be included in one conceptual experience (i.e., included in the foreground of the concept of reality — see Unit of Mentation, Stage Two, in Chapter Two, Mentation), and, second, there is a limit to the speed with which the intellect forms concepts. To solve a complex problem in one step requires an intellectual capacity in excess of either, or both, of these two limitations. One therefore divides the problem into smaller sub-problems that are each within these limitations. Each step in the sequence of abstract concepts is the solution to a sub-problem.

Within a chain of abstract reasoning, each link or concept or sub-solution reflects a separate unit of mentation (see Chapter Two). What such "abstract reasoning" does not reflect (despite its name) is the process of reasoning — one does not experience that process. The real reasoning that is involved in "abstract reasoning" is the three-stage process by which the intellect subdivides the complex problem into specific simpler sub-problems, creates each sub-solution (each of which emerges complete as a separate conceptual experience), and recognizes that the chain is leading from problem to solution.

WILL (CONCENTRATIONAL EXPERIENCES)

Just as concepts are experiences of the intellect, the experiences that one identifies as "concentration" are experiences of the will.

In common usage, the noun "intellect" suggests the existence of a thing that produces intellectual experiences. Similarly, the usage of the term "will" may suggest that there is a thing that produces concentration. However, the constituents of the elemental model of mentality presented in this the book are the elemental experiences themselves. The model does not include an intellect or a will (each with its own elemental existence) that produces the experiences. In this part, the terms "will" and "intellect" refer only to the characteristics of the elemental experiences and not to things with their own characteristics separate from the characteristics of the experiences. Furthermore, the use of the term "will" in this part does not connote "desire," as in the "will to win" or "will to live." Desires are not separate experiences but exist only in the form of the generic behavioral desires included in emotional experiences. One basic function of the will, of concentration, is to implement behavioral desires as part of the mentation process described below in Chapter Two, but the will does not have behavioral desires of its own.

The significance of concentration is this: Only when an element is the subject of concentration is that subject experienced; i.e., only then is one conscious of it, does it form part of reality, does it figure in the decision being made, and will it give rise to a memory. Unless a mental element is the subject of concentration, it will not be experienced in any of these respects (or any other). Only mental elements are subjects of concentration.

The experience of concentration has three properties: direction, magnitude, and frequency. Unlike feelings and intellectual experiences, concentration has no content in addition to these three characteristics.

Characteristics of Concentration

Direction. One experiences the direction of concentration in two ways. First, the subject of concentration (what one is concentrating on) is circumstantial evidence that concentration is focusing in the direction of that subject — the experience that one is experiencing is evidence that concentration is focusing in the direction of that experience. The only subjects of concentration that provide such circumstantial evidence of the direction of concentration are the other elements of mentality (feelings and intellectual experiences). This circumstantial evidence is normally one's principal information concerning the direction of concentration.

Second, in addition to this circumstantial evidence, concentration provides its own proprioceptional evidence of its direction. Ordinary skeletal proprioception is the internal bodily experience that one has of the positions of one's skeletal joints. Skeletal proprioception does not seem to have value. Rather, it seems to be purely informational. One's muscles or skeletal joints can give rise to specific bodily pains (internal bodily experiences with bad value) in particular positions, but even with the body in those painful positions, the proprioceptional sensation has no value. The internal bodily experience of skeletal proprioception seems to be value-neutral. Similarly, concentration has a proprioceptional quality (call it "concentrational proprioception"), which is also value-neutral. The section below concerning outputs describes concentrational proprioception more fully.

The continuous change of subjects of concentration is called the "stream of consciousness."

Magnitude. Magnitude is the intensity of concentration — how hard one is concentrating. One experiences intensity of concentration as the quality identified as effort. Concentrating intensely is called "exerting effort," "exerting will power," or "trying." The will is analogous to an

optical lens in that increasing the intensity of concentration is analogous to increasing the focal length of the lens; i.e., increased intensity
of concentration magnifies the detail of what is in focus but reduces
the angle of view or breadth of the image. A subject of greater concentration will be experienced more singly (with less distraction from
other aspects of present reality) than will a subject of less intense concentration. Although intense concentration over an extended period of
time gives rise to a kind of fatigue, which is an internal bodily input,
concentration itself is value neutral.

Frequency. Frequency of concentration has to do with the number of
changes of subjects of concentration per unit of time, which determines
the number of decisions per unit of time, which is the same as the
number of units of mentation per unit of time. (See Chapter Two,
Mentation.)

These three characteristics of the experiences of the will (direction,
intensity, and frequency) are distinct from feelings or value, particularly
from feelings that can be characterized as a will to behave in a particular
way. The only feelings that carry a behavioral direction are emotions
with their generic behavioral desires. The will does not have a personality of its own exercising its own independent judgment about
behavior. On the contrary, decisions and behavior result in strict logical
relation to feelings current at the time of the decision in the context of
the current concept of reality, as described below in Chapter Two,
Mentation.

The three aspects of concentration are, like breathing, controllable to
some extent. If no effort is made at control, concentrating is self-regu-
lating within the process of mentation. (See Unit of Mentation in
Chapter Two.) But one can decide to pre-empt the self-regulation and
assume a degree of control over all three aspects of concentration. The
difference between self-regulated concentration and decision-directed
concentration is this: Whereas in the former the problem addressed is

simply how to behave, in the latter, the decision responds specifically to a problem concerning the characteristics of concentration. In both cases, concentration follows the decision. (See Unit of Mentation.)

The will does not embody an independent volition just as the steering wheel of a car does not independently direct the behavior of a car. The Introduction to this part provided a functional description of the steering wheel of a car. That description has enough latitude to include such phenomena as the car pulling to the left or right because of a worn tire, or stiffness within the steering system on account of poor lubrication. Similarly, the three characteristics of the will include phenomena such as "states of consciousness." Different states of consciousness can be understood as different modes of concentration, different modes of functioning of the will. In the fully conscious state, the will seems drawn to concentrate on feelings according to their value, and all the elements of mentality are experienced in the process of mentation.

Every state, other than the state of full waking consciousness, involves some kind of constriction on the functioning of the will. In the sleeping state, concentration is only on the intellect (wherein fantasies originate) and on emotions. One is conscious of the fantasy of the dream (an intellectual experience) and of emotional experiences, but one is not conscious of external sensory or internal bodily experiences or outputs. Unconsciousness results from a will that is not concentrating on anything. Hysteria may result from concentration where the intensity does not vary. Catatonia may result where the direction of concentration does not vary. Common "nervousness" can be described as a (mal)function of both intensity and frequency of concentration: intensity and frequency both higher than appropriate in circumstances where relaxation is called for but not high enough where intense concentration and fast thinking are needed — an inability to focus on one subject without distraction for any length of time. The hypnotic state may result when one does not concentrate on emotions. Different trances may be states of consciousness. It is only in the fully conscious state (full waking consciousness) that all the elements are experienced and the model of mentality that this part of the book describes is manifest. These descriptions of states or malfunctions of the will are not intended to be definitive. This part describes only a basic model of mentality in which the basic functions of the elements apply only in full waking consciousness.

The will is a peculiar element in two respects. First, each experience of the will includes the aspects of intensity and direction (effort and concentrational proprioception) that feel like something happening within one's body, and in that sense, experiences of the will resemble internal bodily experiences. Second, the direction, intensity, and frequency of concentration are subject to some degree of control by a decision. To some extent, one can decide on what to concentrate, how hard to concentrate, and how fast to change subjects, and in that sense, the will resembles an output (the subject of the next section).

Outputs and Behavior

The foregoing in this chapter is the full catalogue of the types of elemental mental experiences. There are no other types. One experiences nothing but the types of experiences described above. In order to describe how the basic functions of those elements combine to result in mentation and behavior, I first must describe mental outputs.

Mental outputs are not elemental experiences. I use the term "output" as an abstraction that refers to particular concentrations and particular concepts concerning behavior, as described below.

All mentally caused behavior is reflexive — not involuntary, as with a sneeze, but athletic, as with a complex set of co-ordinated physical movements (such as a grip or grasp) that one performs without specific thought of the individual movements or of how the individual movements are co-ordinated. Such complex co-ordinated physical movements constitute a single reflex, which is caused by the activation of one unit of mental output. Only in the co-ordination of individual muscle contractions is all behavior reflexive or automatic. There are two types of behavior, depending on the way the mental output is activated:

THE ELEMENTAL MODEL OF MENTALITY

learned behavior and instinctive behavior. Each is addressed in turn below.

Learned Outputs and Learned Behavior

The activation of a learned output causes learned behavior. A learned output is activated by its being the subject of concentration in consequence of a decision to direct concentration to focus on that output for the purpose of causing the particular behavior. The ability to direct concentration purposefully to focus on a unit of mental output is learned.

Biofeedback learning of internal bodily control provides a clear demonstration of what learned outputs are and how one learns to focus on them. As an example of a biofeedback device, consider an X-ray machine that provides a continuous, real-time moving image of one's digestive organs. Using the X-ray image, some people are able to control some of the behavior of their digestive organs, of which they would otherwise be unaware.

How does one learn to do this? While viewing the X-ray image, one tries to concentrate on the particular organ. One has no idea what to do or what one is doing, but the biofeedback device signals one that whatever it is that one is concentrating on is correct or incorrect insofar as it produces the desired result or not. The process is entirely one of random experimentation, and when by accident one achieves the desired result (when one sees in the X-ray image the behavior that one is trying to achieve), one tries to duplicate the result by concentrating on whatever it was that gave rise to that result previously. The "it" that one finds to concentrate on that produces the desired result is the particular unit of mental output that causes the appropriate reflexive behavior. The experimentation consists of directing concentration at what can be described only as "unknown territory" until one "finds" the output that gives rise to the desired behavior.

Mental outputs have no experience of their own, and one knows whether an output corresponds to one's intentions only by observing the resultant behavior — like learning to type with neither sight nor feel of the keys but only with sight of the page on which the letters are typed. One has learned the reflex when one has a clear intellectual memory of where to find the corresponding learned output (a memory of the particular direction and intensity of concentration) on which to concentrate at will. It is then part of one's inventory of behavioral skills.

Mental outputs are not themselves elements of mentality; they are not elemental mental experiences. Each output consists of a particular concentration (which is an elemental experience with a particular direction and intensity) and of a concept (an intellectual experience) that the particular direction and intensity of concentration cause a particular bodily behavior. In elemental terms, "behavior" refers not to actual physical behavior but to particular sensory and bodily experiences and to concepts that those experiences connote the behavior of one's body. I use the term "output" purely for ease of description, and the reader can think of it as a mental location on which concentration can focus. An output is defined by a particular direction and intensity of concentration; a reflex is the complex behavior that results from concentration on an output. Hereafter, the complex behavior that results from one mental output unit is called a "behavior" (singular), whereas behavior caused by more than one output is called "behaviors" (plural).

Reflexive behavior resulting from a mental output located initially using biofeedback devices differs from other learned behavior only in that mechanical sensing devices assisted in learning the former but not the latter.

Learned behaviors result from concentration on learned outputs. Chapter Two explains that concentration does not focus on a learned output except in consequence of a purposeful decision to behave. Consequently, learned behavior can also be called "decision-directed," as opposed to instinctive behavior, which is genuinely automatic.

Instinctive Outputs and Instinctive Behavior

Instinctive behavior is also reflexive. For example, when one exerts great muscular effort (an internal bodily feeling and intense concentration), one automatically grimaces (behavior resulting from a grimace output), quite apart from any decision to grimace or from any thought or decision relating to the many complex movements that, in the aggregate, constitute a grimace. "Grimace" is a vague term that includes the many different facial expressions of a number of bad feelings. It may be that each feeling has its own specific reflex. Certainly, some feelings have specific reflexes, and, like the feelings that give rise to reflexes, each reflex has a spectrum of intensities, so that the intensity of the reflex will be proportionate to the intensity of the feeling giving rise to the reflex. For example, the feeling of muscular effort may be slight or extreme, and so the resultant grimace will vary accordingly from slight to extreme. A slightly grimacing face looks quite different from an extremely grimacing face, and the physiology may be different, but both types of behavior constitute the same reflex caused by the same unit of mental output, the difference being one of intensity. Whether or not each feeling is associated with unique instinctive reflexive behavior, each feeling is associated with only one instinctive behavior. The experience of a feeling seems automatically to cause its associated instinctive reflexive behavior. Purely for ease of description, I say that a feeling activates an instinctive output that causes the particular instinctive behavior.

Instinctive reflexes reflect feelings, occur without learning or intention, and constitute an inherent and universal language of feelings in the form of particular facial expressions, tones of voice, postures, and so on. These types of behavior can be caused only by a genuine experience of the associated feeling. One can intentionally mimic instinctive reflexes, and some people are better actors than others (see below, Acting, in Chapter Two), but the counterfeit behavior appears subtly different and feels completely different subjectively.

General Characteristics of Outputs and Behavior
- Outputs have no feeling, no value, no signature experience whatever, and are not elemental experiences. "Concentration on an output" is shorthand for a particular direction and intensity of concentration that one expects will result in particular behavior. Similarly, "bodily

behavior" is shorthand for particular external sensory and internal bodily experiences and intellectual experiences that interpret those feelings as the behavior of one's body. Also as shorthand, the abstraction "output" can be considered a mental location on which concentration can focus.

- All behavior is analyzable into complex behaviors, each of which results from the activation of an individual mental output. The plural term "behaviors" refers to behavior that results from the activation of more than one mental output unit.

- Instinctive outputs are universal, as is the potential inventory of learned outputs. One develops one's individual inventory of learned outputs, which one has available to activate by a decision to do so.

- Chapter Two shows that learned (decision-directed) behavior proceeds *seriatim* (one reflex at a time), whereas instinctive types of behavior can occur simultaneously, as though superimposed on each other.

- To learn a behavioral skill is to conceptualize the mental location of the appropriate output, so that a decision to behave in a skillful way is a decision to activate an appropriate output by concentrating in a particular direction with a particular intensity.

- Each output has specific complex behavior associated with it (variable only according to intensity). One could learn the individual motor movements that together amount to, for example, a jump or a grip/grasp, but one could never co-ordinate the individual execution of all those individual movements into a jump or a grip/grasp (far too complex). One can, however, effectively combine different reflexes by learning a new output that, when activated, causes the aggregate of combined reflexes.

CHAPTER TWO

MENTATION

UNIT OF MENTATION

C HAPTER One identified the five families of elemental mental experiences (the elements of mentality): external sensory experiences, internal bodily experiences, emotions, intellectual experiences, and concentrations. In normal waking life, one's experiences do not occur in a random or chaotic manner. Rather, they follow a cyclical pattern caused by their interrelating functions. This cyclical organization is mentation. Each cycle within the organization is a unit of mentation. Normal waking life is divided into units of mentation, and the experiences within each unit are sub-divided into five stages.

This chapter addresses the organization of experiences within a unit of mentation. The organization of sequential units is addressed below in this chapter in the section Mentation: The Sequence of Units.

The five stages within a unit of mentation are as follows:

    stage 1: external sensory and internal bodily experiences
        (pre-emptive hierarchy of feelings)
    stage 2: concept of reality (interpretation of the experiences in stage 1)
    stage 3: emotions (hierarchy of generic behavioral desires)

stage 4: concept how to behave (decision)
stage 5: concentration on learned output (implementation
of decision)

An experience becomes so by being the subject of concentration. Therefore a sequence of experiences (including the organized sequence that constitutes mentation) reflects a sequence of subjects of concentration and a corresponding sequence of directions of concentration. The properties of the different types of elements are functional properties and give rise to the basic functions of the elements. To drive the sequential change of direction of concentration is the generic function of all experiences. I describe below how each stage of mentation drives concentration to change direction so as to lead to the next stage.

Stage 1: External Sensory and Internal Bodily Experiences. These experiences are feelings and hence include value. Concentration has three aspects: direction, intensity, and frequency. Direction is indicated by the subject of concentration, the experience of which one is conscious at the time. The more intense a feeling (the greater its value), the more intense will be the resultant concentration on that feeling. A situation involving different experiences with different magnitudes of value results in a hierarchy, whereby those experiences with greatest magnitude of value become subjects of most intense concentration, and those with least magnitude of value become subjects of very weak concentration and may not be noticed at all.

This hierarchy of sensory and bodily experiences according to their value is experienced as an intrusion into the stream of concentration. Thus, for example, a flash of bright light will intrude into concentration and pre-empt the fantasy of a daydream, but the flash might itself be pre-empted by the pain of being struck by lightning. The pre-emptive hierarchy is a mechanism that sorts sensory and bodily experiences into an order that is appropriate to one's relation to the external world. The term "pre-emptive hierarchy" describes the relationship between each sensory and bodily experience and the will whereby the value of each feeling directs concentration to focus on it with intensity proportionate to its value by intruding into consciousness and demanding to be dealt with proportionately. The pre-emptive hierarchy also describes the importance attached to the respective experiences in reaching a decision (see stage 4).

Within one unit of mentation (i.e., within the present), sensory and bodily experiences seem to occur simultaneously and continuously. For example, one can discern visually numerous events within the time span of a single unit of mentation. Therefore, it may seem incorrect to describe a unit of mentation as containing only one visual experience. However, only once per unit of mentation (in stage 2) is sensory experience intellectually conceptualized. The visual experience that is conceptualized at stage 2 of a unit of mentation is the full content of all visual experience since the last conceptualization, which occurred in stage 2 of the previous unit. The concept that one creates to make sense of all sensory experience within a unit of mentation may contain ideas of numerous sequential events and even of time divisible into infinitesimally small points. One can create that concept of it, however, only once per unit of mentation. The present has the duration of one unit — the elemental present is not a mathematical point of no duration. The visual events that are, *ex post facto*, conceived to have been several events occurring within the unit constitute one visual experience containing a temporally organized quantity of visual data.

This is the key to resolving the issue that was raised at the beginning of Chapter One: how to distinguish an experience of one type from its immediate predecessor or successor of the same type. All intellectual experiences emerge complete. Successive intellectual experiences, therefore, are inherently discrete. For other types of experiences, there may or may not be sharp, discrete distinctions between successive experiences, but one can conceive that distinction only once per unit of mentation in stage 2. Therefore, for the purpose of understanding the organization of experiences that constitute mentation, it does not matter whether or not successive experiences of a particular type within one unit are discretely separate or continuous — the totality of any particular type of experience within one unit is considered to be one experience that is discretely separate from others of the same type that occurred within prior, or will occur within subsequent, units of mentation. For other purposes, it may be useful to make finer distinctions.

The previous paragraphs illustrate how quickly the content of sensory experiences (stage 1) can change in comparison to speed of conceptualization (stage 2): conceiving what sensory experiences mean normally occurs in the range of one or two times per second, but, within the time separating successive concepts, sensory content can change many times. For instance, one can discern a pinball bouncing numerous times before one can conceive what has happened. However, some sensory experiences are anomalous in that they seem to interfere with the fine-grained agility of sensory experiences to change content rapidly. For example, a bright light, a loud sound, a strong, foul taste all seem to leave lingering after-sights, after-sounds, and after-tastes, which I call "ghosts." One learns to recognize that these ghosts do not represent separate sensory content of their own referable to the present but rather are after-effects that reflect experiences from an earlier unit. This is a kind of leakage between consecutive units of mentation. Feelings may leak from one unit to the next, but intellectual experiences do not. Each unit of mentation is discretely separate from its predecessor and its successor in that each of the three has its own concept of reality in stage 2 and its own concept of how to behave in stage 4. Reality is conceived separately and anew within each unit, even though the concept of reality may contain the content that some sensory experience is the ghost of experiences in preceding units. (For "speed of mentation," see Mentation: The Sequence of Units, below.)

Nevertheless, purely for purposes of diagrammatic illustration, a simplified model of mentality is described below that treats sensory and bodily experiences as occurring *seriatim* within a unit of mentation, as though the focus of concentration scanned these experiences *seriatim*, and as though the illusion of continuity and simultaneity of sensory and bodily experiences were analogous to the illusion of a motion picture, which is actually composed of serially organized, individual still pictures.

The first stage within each unit of mentation is the hierarchy of present external sensory and internal bodily experiences arranged in order of their value. The values of the experiences in the first phase draw concentration to focus on the experiences with intensity of concentration proportionate to their relative values and drive the intellect to interpret the experiences — to create a concept that logically relates the present sensory and bodily experiences to all other concepts. The value of present experiences draws one's attention and automatically poses the problem: "What's drawing my attention?" Stage 1 poses the problem that the intellect solves in stage 2. The problem "What's drawing my attention?" is more properly styled "What's reality?", or just "Conceive reality!"

Stage 2: Interpretation of Phase 1 Experiences: Concept of Present Reality. The values of the experiences in the first stage of mentation drive the intellect to interpret them — to create a concept that relates the experiences of phase 1 to all concepts. That interpretation is the concept of present reality. The problem "What's drawing my attention?" posed in stage 1 leads to the solution "concept of present reality" in stage 2. Within every unit of mentation, one conceives present reality anew by creating a new concept that logically relates present sensory and bodily experiences to all of one's concepts by revising or updating the immediate past concept of reality. Stage 1 drives the intellect to solve the "reality problem" that the values of the experiences in stage 1 pose to the intellect. (The intellect has no self-motivation to solve problems.) The solution to the reality problem (the concept of reality) is the first of two intellectual creations within one unit of mentation, and the second is the decision how to behave, which is experienced in stage 4.

At some fairly early period in one's life, one develops a working concept of three-dimensional physical reality, of the hierarchical structure of time, and of causal relations between some prior and some subsequent physical phenomena. These very general concepts give rise to the normal working interpretation of external reality, what is called "objective physical reality" (see Practical Physical Reality in Chapter Three). At some point, one's concept of present reality comes to include the notion of one's past and potential futures (at that point, present reality has the illusory quality of temporal depth (or movement through time), whereby one understands what one calls "the past" to have preceded the present and the present to be moving into the future). The concept of a particular potential future includes some information concerning both the value that one would expect to experience if that potential future should occur and the contingent, causal relationship between that potential future and one's behavior in the interim (the period between the present and that point in the future).

In addition to taking on the illusions of spatial and temporal "depth," one's practical working concept of reality acquires the characteristics of foreground and background — the illusion of theatrical stage-depth. Dealing with reality is an economic enterprise in which the currency is the inherent value of feelings. Every aspect of one's concept of reality includes its logical connection to value. Some aspects of one's concept of reality will have more direct connection to greater value than will others. Those with closer connection to value are called "important" and constitute the foreground of one's concept of reality. Those with less become unimportant background details.

One's concept of reality is composed of numerous constituent concepts organized in a hierarchy of importance whereby the most important concepts occupy the foreground, the less important concepts occupy the mid-ground, and the unimportant background containing unimportant concepts may not be noticed. In total, the concepts composing the fore-, mid-, and backgrounds of one's concept of present reality exhaust one's entire intellectual inventory. One's entire inventory of concepts is included in the concept of present reality within each unit of mentation, and the apparent radical difference between one concept of reality and the next derives from different stage-depth organizations of those numerous constituent concepts reflecting different relative importance attached to each constituent within different units rather than different constituents. The reference to fore-, mid-, and backgrounds is not intended to suggest that the hierarchy of importance contains three discrete echelons. On the contrary, there may be many echelons, but the most important, the foreground, stands out with

greatest detail, and the less important contain less detail — detail propor-
tionate to importance. The stage-depth hierarchical organization reflects
the limit of total intellectual detail that can be contained in one intellec-
tual experience.

As an illustration of stage-depth dimensionality, consider a road map of a
city of modest size. One can regard the map as a grid of streets in which
the shape of the entire grid is in the foreground of one's interpretation of
the visual experience of the map, and none of the streets stands out from
the others; or one might identify a few main streets or intersections in
which case those landmarks stand out from the rest, which are relegated to
background; or one might identify a particular address on a minor street in
which case that address stands out and everything else on the map is rele-
gated to background. The visual experience of the map might contain
sufficient visual information to enable the identification of every address on
every street and every other macroscopic or microscopic feature of the city,
but one does not have the intellectual capacity to create one concept con-
taining all of that detailed intellectual information in the foreground.
Consequently, one creates a hierarchy whereby the most important informa-
tion stands out with greatest detail in the foreground of one's interpretation
of the map, and the less important information occupies the background
with less detail. Whatever concepts occupy the foreground, they are called
the "subject" of the concept of reality, and the organization of the remainder
(the mid- and backgrounds) is called the "context" in which the subject is
experienced.

But if an address on a map is the subject of a concept of reality, the context
does not end at the borders of the map. In deeper background than the
edge of the map is one's concept explaining how one finds oneself looking
at a map and why. But even these concepts are experienced in the context
of concepts yet farther in the background, concepts of oneself and one's
relation to other people and physical reality. Even the concepts of physical
reality and one's relation to other people stand in the context of concepts
farther back yet — concepts distinguishing external sensory experiences
from other types of experiences (the interpretation of external sensory expe-
riences constitutes one's concept of external physical reality). The concepts

THE ELEMENTAL MODEL OF MENTALITY

that distinguish one type of elemental experience from another constitute one's elemental model of mentality — the deepest background. No matter what the subject of one's concept of reality, the context of that subject consists of a conceptual structure of which the base — the deepest background, the intellectual foundation — is one's elemental model of mentality. In this way, the entire inventory of concepts is included in one's concept of reality.

The simplest city might be a right-angle grid of streets. In such a city, one can travel directly from, for example, the northeast corner to the southeast corner without passing through the center of town. The layout of one's intellectual inventory, however, is more like a hub and spokes than like a grid — some concepts are directly related to one another, but many are only related through the hub. The model of mentality is analogous to a hub through which any concept is related to any other.

At the conclusion of stage 2, one experiences a concept of reality that is multi-dimensional and detailed. It has spatial dimensionality, defining three-dimensional space and one's present location ("location" here includes all the present physical attributes of all physical things organized in order of importance, including one's body). It has temporal dimensionality, recognizing the present to be a point on the temporal hierarchy and present physical reality to be both a logical consequence (the effect) of the past and the cause of the future. Temporal detail may include features of optional futures, including the particular behavior that one would have to adopt in the interim to cause particular futures to be realized and including also the value that one would expect in each of those optional futures. It has stage-depth dimensionality: Every detail of the concept is ordered in a hierarchy of importance (connection to value), whereby important details stand out in the foreground and unimportant details may be so far in the background as not to be noticed.

Thus stage 1 poses the reality problem to which the concept of present reality in stage 2 is the solution. The concept of present reality is the first intellectual creation within one unit of mentation, and it contains concepts that cause emotions that form stage 3. Thus the conclusion of stage 2 drives the mentation process into stage 3.

Stage 3: Emotions. The concept of reality created in stage 2 contains concepts that give rise to emotions, which are experienced in stage 3.

Each emotional experience includes a strategic behavioral desire. The functional significance of an emotional desire is to direct (to drive) concentration to change direction from focusing on the emotional experience to focusing on the intellect in order to solve the second problem within the unit: to determine the specific behavior to best implement the generic strategic desire. (Call this the "problem of specific behavior," in which one seeks "specific behavior" to deal with a particular reality, as opposed to "strategic" or "generic" desires, which apply to any reality.) Each emotional experience poses a problem of specific behavior for the intellect to solve in the context of the particular concept of reality at that time.

Simultaneous experiences of different emotions of various intensities give rise to a hierarchy ordered according to the magnitude of the value of each. Each emotion includes an inherent behavioral strategic desire (for example, fear includes the behavioral strategic desire to sprint away from the danger). The hierarchy of emotional experiences implies a hierarchy of strategic behavioral desires.

Of all types of experiences, only emotions carry behavioral directions, which one experiences as a desire to behave according to a particular generic strategy. The other types of feelings (external sensory and internal bodily experiences) intrude into the stream of consciousness according to their value, but they are neutral as to behavior. For example, a sharp pain in the hand has bad value but does not alone direct one what to do about it. However, the knowledge that the pain is caused by a biting insect (including the knowledge of what an insect is, of the significance of the bite, and of behavioral options) gives rise to an intellectual definition of present reality leading to anger or horror or other emotions, which do carry strategic desires concerning how one should behave with respect to the biting insect.

Similarly, hunger, a bodily experience, does not carry a behavioral direction. One's intellectual understanding of hunger, however, includes two ideas: (1) that food tastes better with greater intensity of hunger than with less intense hunger (i.e., hunger, an internal bodily experience, gives rise to a shift in the value of tastes, which are external sensory experiences), and (2) that hunger dissipates with eating. These ideas give rise to emotions. In the aggregate, the bodily experience of hunger, the two ideas, and the resulting emotions constitute one's appetite. When one is hungry, it is the emotions involved in one's appetite, not the internal bodily experience of hunger, that contain the behavioral directions. One's sexual appetite is the aggregate of the internal bodily experience of sexual arousal, concepts that the bodily experience connotes a shift in the value of particular external sensory experiences, and emotions that are evoked by those concepts. Once again, the emotions involved in one's sexual appetite, rather than the internal bodily experience of sexual arousal, contain the behavioral directions.

Where the concept of present reality includes concepts of optional futures including the expected values of those futures, those concepts generate emotions, as does any other aspect of the concept of present reality. The emotions generated by a concept of a bad future include strategic desires to avoid that future. Conversely, the emotions generated by a concept of a good future include strategic desires to achieve it.

Where one experiences various emotions within one unit of mentation, each emotion includes its own generic behavioral desire and poses its own problem of specific behavior, but the intellect can provide only one solution for all the present specific problems — one can behave only one way at a time. The one solution to all the problems is experienced in stage 4. That solution — the decision — is the second concept experienced within the unit. Thus the functional characteristics of the elements experienced in stage 3 drive the mentation process to stage 4.

Commonly, sensory experiences demonstrate fine-grained agility in the rapid change of content. Nevertheless, one understands some of them to be ghosts lingering from previous units of mentation (see stage 1). In contrast with sensory experiences, emotions are not characterized by rapid change but notoriously linger well after the concept giving rise to them has changed. The concept of great danger quickly causes great fear, but the fear does not immediately vanish when one conceives that the danger has passed. Emotions commonly subside slowly and leak into subsequent units of mentation.

When an emotional ghost leaks from the unit in which it was caused by its specific concept into subsequent units in which the specific concept does not occur, the ghost (1) is experienced as part of stage 1 in the subsequent unit and (2) may or may not be understood to be a ghost rather than a separate experience, with its own present conceptual cause, but (3) it nevertheless includes its own value and strategic desire and (4) will figure in the decision being made in exactly the same way as if it were caused by a present concept — as if it were not a ghost. Even though sensory and emotional ghosts may be a kind of leakage from one unit of mentation to subsequent units, each unit contains a unique concept of reality that makes sense of all present experiences.

Stage 4: The Decision How to Behave. Where one experiences a number of emotions within one unit of mentation, a number of strategic behavioral desires are included, and they may conflict. Where there are multiple emotions experienced simultaneously with different intensities, the strategic desires are ordered hierarchically according to the magnitude of the value of each emotion. Thus stages 1, 2, and 3 define present reality and provide an ordered list of distinct strategies that one desires to implement in order to deal with the present reality.

The hierarchy of strategic behavioral desires included in present emotional experiences constitutes instructions to (drives) one's intellect to determine the one behavior to maximally implement all the desired strategies — to decide in what direction and with what intensity to focus concentration so as to cause the one learned behavior (from one's inventory of learned behaviors) that maximally implements all the ordered generic behavioral desires within the context of present reality. How do I do what I want to do here and now? The one solution to the aggregate of specific problems of behavior is the decision. There is one decision per unit of mentation, and it is the second concept created within each unit. The decision is an intellectual determination of the one behavior, out of the many represented by one's whole inventory of decision-directed outputs, that maximally implements all the distinct ordered emotional desires — "maximally," because strategies lower in the hierarchy may be ignored in deference to more intensely desired strategies. The calculation of the one learned behavior that maximally implements all the different desires with different intensities attaches greater weight to those desires with greater intensity than to those with less. The branch of mathematics called "game theory" uses the type of logic involved in the maximal calculation.

Beneficently, the totality of strategic behavioral desires inherent in emotions, in conjunction with concepts of potential futures that are dependent on one's behavior in the interim, seems to be purposefully designed to maximize value for oneself. Posing the problem "How do I do what I want to do here and now?" is equivalent to asking "How do I maximize value?"

The decision results from the mechanical computation of the intellect in much the same way as the computer-controlled fuel-injection system of a modern car takes several factors into account and "decides" to make the fuel mixture richer rather than leaner. This "mechanical computation" is the creative product of the intellect, but that is not to imply that the intellect has its own independent personality. On the contrary, the intellect appears strictly to follow its inherent logic, just as a computer strictly follows its instructions.

Habits represent an abbreviated type of decision-making process. Intentional behavior is immediately preceded by decisions that cause it. Experiments in reaction time have attempted to determine minimum decision-making times. Those experiments were designed so that most of the intellectual work involved in the decision had been done and the subject of the experiment did not have to figure out afresh within each unit of mentation where he fitted into external reality or what to do. The subject had been fully instructed that as soon as the gun fired, he was to commence sprinting down the track.

This example illustrates a whole category of decisions called "habitual." From the perspective of an external observer, a habit is simply repetitive behavior, but subjectively, habitual behavior results when, in consequence of training, part of the decision-making process is already done — i.e., once the intellectual work of conceiving the present circumstances is completed, the reasoning capability of the intellect automatically chooses the preconceived habitual behavior without going through the whole maximal implementation computation to determine the best behavior. Habits, then, result where the intellect renders a preconceived decision rather than a newly reasoned one. The abbreviated reasoning process that habits demonstrate is probably responsible for the great majority of daily decisions. So long as the habitual behavior is appropriate, the more abbreviated the process, the better. Throughout most of human evolution, decision-making speed has probably been more important than philosophical rigor. Bad habits, however, are not beneficent. Where a bad habit is operative, asking "How do I do what I want to do here and now?" is not equivalent to asking "How do I get most value?"

Any reasoning (not simply deciding on behavior) may be abbreviated in this way. For example, one learns the tables for addition and then is able habitually to conclude that one plus one equals two, and so on, without reasoning those conclusions afresh each time.

Stage 5: Implementation of Decision: Outputs. Once one decides what to do, what output to activate, concentration automatically adopts the direction and intensity that have been decided. The decision in stage 4 to activate an output is itself an instruction to the will to activate that output in stage 5. One experiences no intermediate step. Concentration on an output automatically follows a decision to do so. A decision to activate an output, without more, results in concentration on that output as instructed. There are no intermediate steps, no reconsideration or confirmation, before the decision is implemented by concentration focusing obediently. Thus the decision in stage 4 drives the activation of an output that occurs in stage 5.

In stage 5, the only thing that one experiences is the effort and direction of concentration focusing, as instructed, on one output.

Just as a number of visual or auditory events may seem to occur within one unit of mentation, so one output may involve a number of consecutive co-ordinated output events (see stage 1).

But no sooner has an output been activated (stage 5) than newly present feelings intrude into the stream of consciousness and demand to be dealt with; thus stage 1 of the next unit of mentation commences, *et seq.*

This description of a unit of mentation might seem to apply only to the first units of mentation that occur when one awakens and concentration focuses on whatever sensory or bodily experience is most valuable with no reference to whatever occurred before. However, within a few seconds after awakening, "one finds one's bearings," and the foreground of the sequential concepts of reality over successive units of mentation seems to maintain a purposeful continuity. For example, while one is reading a book, the foreground of the successive concepts of reality continually consists of the page of the book and the concepts derived from the words on the page. This continuity does not occur because the visual experiences of the page are significantly more beautiful (have more value) any other sensory or bodily experiences. Rather, the continuity occurs because each decision made in stage 4 while one is reading contains a behavioral instruction to the will to concentrate on the page within stage 5.

Consequently, when stage 1 of the next unit occurs, the sensory experiences that constitute the page will be higher in the pre-emptive hierarchy than the background not because the page is more beautiful than the background but because concentration has implemented the decision in the previous unit. (For decision-directed concentration, see The Will in Chapter One.) While reading, the purposeful continuity of successive units of mentation derives from successive decisions, each of which includes a behavioral instruction to continue to maintain concentration on the page to achieve the purpose of reading. But despite such a decision, concentration on the page is always liable to pre-emption by the intrusion of a significantly more valuable sensory or bodily experience. Each unit of mentation is subdivided into five stages as described above whether or not the decision contains an instruction with respect to concentration — whether there is a purposeful continuity between successive units or whether stage 1 contains no reference to what occurred previously.

DIAGRAMMATIC REPRESENTATION

This completes the description of the elements of mentality and how their basic functions interrelate within a unit of mentation. An abstract diagrammatic representation of a simplified model of mentality may now be helpful.

Let the points on a circle represent all possible locations on which concentration can focus. The circle then represents the universe of potential subjective experience.

Numbers of television monitors are positioned along the arc and face the centre of the circle. The monitors are grouped in four areas representing four types of elemental experiences (external sensory experiences, internal bodily experiences, emotions, and concepts).

First, the segment of arc from twelve o'clock to two o'clock represents external sensory experiences. Positioned along this segment are seven monitors representing the seven types of external sensory experiences (visual, auditory, gustatory, olfactory, tactile, acceleratory, and rhythmic). The brightness of each monitor represents the intensity of the experience, and the color, red or blue, represents its goodness or its badness, respectively. The detail on the monitor represents the remaining content of the experience.

Second, along the segment of arc from two o'clock to four o'clock is an array of monitors representing internal bodily experiences. Again, the brightness and color displayed on each monitor represent intensity and value, and the detail represents the remaining content.

Third, along the arc from four o'clock to six o'clock, an array of twenty-two monitors represents emotions. These monitors are arranged in eleven pairs. The pairs are set up like bunk beds, with one member above and the other below. The eleven "above" members are red, those below, blue. Each screen represents a particular emotion and has the appropriate label. The brightness of the display on these monitors also connotes intensity of the experience, and the color, red or blue, its goodness or badness. There is, however, no variation in the picture on each of these screens, no variation in the content. Other than the intensity and value of its specific feeling, the content of an emotional experience is only its strategic desire. Therefore these monitors are small.

Fourth, along the segment from six o'clock to nine o'clock, one large monitor represents the intellect. This monitor is large enough to display a full range of conceptual detail including the hierarchical structure of knowledge described in Chapter Three, the multi-dimensional concept of reality occurring in stage 2 of the unit of mentation and the behavioral decision in stage 4. The inferred intellectual functions of reasoning and knowledge are not subjects of concentration and are not experienced and so do not appear on the intellectual monitor. Only concepts appear (including perhaps the concept that there is an intellect that reasons and also acquires, stores, and retrieves concepts). This monitor's brightness is comparatively weak and does not vary, nor does it display any color.

Fifth, the remaining segment of the circle, from nine o'clock to twelve o'clock, is the output area. It has neither monitors nor anything else that can be illuminated. When concentration focuses on an output, no experience results. Accordingly, the appropriate symbol is a blank area that contains numerous invisible sensors. The sensors are divided into two groups representing instinctive and learned outputs. A sensor representing a learned output is activated only when concentration focuses precisely on that output — even then that sensor is not illuminated, because without some external sensory or internal bodily information, one does not know on what output, if any, one is concentrating.

If the circle drawn on the page represents the universe of subjective experience, the will would be in the center of the circle. A mechanism that would analogize some of the characteristics of the will would be a focusing spotlight on a swivel base that would allow the spotlight to illuminate any point on the arc. By this analogy, the stream of consciousness is made up of the continuous change of monitors along the arc that are illuminated by the spotlight. In this simplest analogy, a unit of mentation is one rotation of the spotlight, during which it focuses on each of the other elements and creates an illusion of continuity and simultaneity by the frequency of rotations. In the full five-stage process of mentation, the intellect is experienced twice (in stages 2 and 4), and so the idea of rotational units (however appealing) may be simplistic. The idea of sensory events (plural) and sequential outputs within one unit also introduces difficulties for this diagram.

Emotional ghosts imply the possibility of emotions in the present unit of mentation reflecting concepts in a preceding unit. These emotional ghosts (including their behavioral desires) are experienced in stage 1. This possibility suggests the further possibility that, within one unit of mentation, the intellect need be canvassed only once to conceive both reality and how best to implement strategic desires. If so, it might not be simplistic to represent a unit of mentation as a rotational sequence in which concentration focuses seriatim *on feelings (external sensory experiences, internal bodily experiences, and emotions), on the intellect (where the concept of reality and the decision occur consecutively), and on outputs,* et seq.

The spotlight has some type of focal length or zoom control that can change the beam of light from narrowly focused and intense to broadly diffused. This control would be labeled "intensity of concentration." The spotlight also has another control mechanism to govern the state of consciousness. Clearly, "on" and "off" are analogous to "conscious" and "unconscious," but there are intermediate possibilities representing other states. Since direction, intensity, and frequency of concentration are also experienced, the swiveling spotlight is represented by a monitor positioned near the segment of arc representing bodily experiences. This monitor is divided into three sections representing the three aspects of the experience of concentration. Furthermore, since one can, to some extent, control the three aspects of concentration by decisions, the spotlight is also represented by appropriate sensors within the output area on the arc.

The elemental experiences are represented by images on the monitors on the arc, and the functional properties of the elements are represented in the diagram by something analogous to "wiring" (lines connecting the elements). For example, emotions are connected to the intellect in such a way that concentration on a particular intellectual concept gives rise to a particular emotional experience. This connection, therefore, is represented on the diagram by a line from the intellectual screen to each emotional monitor. Each feeling monitor is connected by a line to a particular instinctive output to illustrate that concentration on a feeling activates the appropriate instinctive output that is part of the instinctive language of feelings. Particular bodily experiences (such as hunger) are connected to particular external sensory experiences (such as taste). All the connections between the elements outlined above (the basic connections) are represented in the diagram by the analogy of wiring. The wires are drawn on the diagram but are colored to indicate that the connections are functionally present but do not represent experience. Only the displays on the monitors represent experiences.

MENTATION: THE SEQUENCE OF UNITS

The frequency of mentation is in the range of one or two units of mentation per second. Thus a unit of mentation within a pattern of continuous mentation lasts about one or one-half second (called the "period" of mentation), although mentation may sometimes be much faster or slower. In Chapter One, frequency was described as a characteristic or property of concentration. "Frequency of concentration" is synonymous with "frequency of mentation." In the diagrammatic representation of mentality, frequency of concentration or of mentation would be represented by the number of rotations of concentration within a unit of time. During one rotation, the direction of concentration canvasses all the elements in the five stages within one unit of mentation.

The period of mentation is the duration of what is called the "present." The elemental present is not a point of infinitesimal duration.

Much of life proceeds at a leisurely pace in which the "stream of consciousness" seems seamless, fluid. At a leisurely pace, each element of mentality seems represented by its own stream of consciousness, and all the streams seem to be simultaneous as well as seamless. However, it is the contention of this book that life is not fluid but, like a motion picture, is composed of discrete units of mentation, each made up of distinct, separate stages.

Sometimes the discreteness of the sequential stages of mentation is evident. In almost any athletic-type event involving speed, technique, and tactics, as one approaches the high-frequency limit of one's mentation, the distinction between one unit and the next becomes apparent. One is aware not only of the time between successive decisions (successive mentation units) but of the time within a unit of mentation — for example, the time between the sensory experiences and their interpretation, between the interpretation and the decision, and between the decision and its implementation. Furthermore, at one's high-frequency limit, time seems to stand still in each phase. At the upper limit, one concentrates as intensely as possible — first, on figuring out where one is and what is happening; second, on figuring out what to do; third, on doing it — on and on.

The two intellectual functions (the interpretation of the sensory experiences and the decision) occur distinctly and in that order. During high-speed mentation, the feelings (external sensory experiences, internal bodily experiences, and emotions) may also seem discontinuous. The apparent continuity and simultaneity of experiences within the stream of consciousness during mentation at common speeds may be an illusion like a motion picture. My estimate of high-frequency mentation is in the order of four units per second.

The following describes an experiment to measure the highest speed of mentation. Consider an electronic game in which the apparatus consists of a computer monitor divided into four quadrants (upper and lower, left and right) and a control device with left and right buttons. During the course of the game, one quadrant at a time is illuminated. When illuminated, the two quadrants on the left side are colored red and the two on the right are blue. On the control device, the left button is colored red, and the right is blue. When the game begins, one of the upper quadrants is illuminated, and it remains illuminated for one second. The duration of the illumination is called the "period" of the point. The subject of the experiment does not know, before the period begins, whether the left-upper or right-upper quadrant will be illuminated, and he scores a point if, during the period, he depresses the button (left or right) that corresponds with the side that is illuminated. When the period ends, whichever upper quadrant was illuminated ceases to be illuminated, and one of the lower quadrants becomes illuminated for the same period as the previous illumination. The subject scores a point during this second period if he depresses the left or right button corresponding to the lower quadrant that is illuminated. The third period is similar to the first. The game consists of alternating upper and lower points for which the periods are constant and predictable, but the subject cannot predict for any point whether the left or right quadrant will be illuminated because the computer is programmed so that the left or right illumination is purely random. The game continues as long as the subject depresses only the correct button within each period. The game ends when the subject does not depress only the correct button within a period, and then the score for that game is the total number of correct depressions. The game consists of phases. Each phase lasts ten seconds. There is no pause between phases. In the first phase, the period for each point is one second. In each subsequent phase, the period is reduced by twenty-five percent of the period in the previous phase (or perhaps some larger or smaller percentage).

For each point, the subject must conceive a new reality, the important aspect of which could not have been predicted, and then he must decide on a course of behavior, and then he must implement the decision. Each point represents a separate unit of mentation. The experiment is designed to minimize the conceptual and behavioral difficulty of each stage so that the period at the end of the game represents maximum speed of mentation. At the conclusion of the game, the maximum speed of mentation (the number of units of mentation per unit of time) would be represented by the inverse of the period of the last fully completed stage.

For the subject playing the game at maximum speed, the foreground of his concept of reality consists of the elements of the game. But the elements of the game involve no motivation, no emotion in themselves. Why does the subject continue with the game? Even though the foreground of the subject's concept of reality is occupied with the elements of the game, the background consists of the subject's self-concept and his concept of the external world including the other humans with whom he is socially involved. (In deep background is his model of mentality and how external and social reality is constructed from mental elements.) It is the social context that provides the motivation. The game may seem to the subject fully to occupy his attention, but within each unit of mentation, reality entire is conceived, and it is the conceptual background that gives rise to emotions with behavioral desires. The depression of the button to earn each point is behavior chosen by the subject within that unit of mentation to maximally implement the hierarchy of emotional behavioral desires experienced within that unit in consequence of the background within the overall concept of reality unique to that unit, all for the purpose of maximizing value.

At the leisurely pace of normal life, one has sufficient intellectual capacity to cope with immediate requirements (such as the athletic adjustments involved in walking), and one may have sufficient additional intellectual capacity to enjoy the fantasy of a daydream that involves a sequence of intellectual and emotional experiences that are fully integrated with the reality of walking but seem separate in terms of foreground/background. It is the frequency of mentation that makes the experiences seem fluid and simultaneous and yet separate. An athlete performing at his high-frequency limit may look gracefully fluid to an observer, but the athlete experiences distinct phases in which time almost seems to stand still. When performing at one's limit one has no excess mental capacity. If one should concentrate on a fantasy or anything other than the business at hand, the stream of consciousness would contain abrupt discontinuities. While performing at one's high-frequency limit, one dedicates one's intellectual capacity to processing only immediate sensory and bodily experiences.

Mentation involving only present sensory and bodily experiences (as opposed to memories or fantasies, which involve concepts pertinent to the past) is called "spontaneity," the "transcendental experience," "living in the present," "going with the flow," and so on. This situation obtains, for example, at maximum speed in serious athletic-type circumstances, at minimum speed in meditation, and at an intermediate speed in watching an engaging movie. There is a great deal of folklore surrounding this type of mentation, but it has no special value in itself; its only value is that of the feelings generated, which may be good or bad. This type of mentation represents a state in which the frequency of mentation (the number of units of mentation per unit of time) is exactly sufficient to deal with present sensory and bodily reality without accompanying fantasies.

ACTING

Decisions respond to feelings, and decision-directed behavior is most often accompanied by observable instinctive behavior caused directly by the feelings giving rise to the decision. Whatever one decides to do, one's tone of voice, facial expressions, postures, and so on are indicators of how one feels, and this dichotomy (between simultaneous instinctive behavior and decision-directed behavior) obtains even when one's decision is to behave as though one were experiencing different feelings. Intentional learned behavior that is intended to mimic instinctive behavior is called "acting."

The language of feelings consists of specific facial expressions, tones of voice, postures, and so on, which I call "instinctive mannerisms" and these mannerisms are universal. One is acting when one intentionally

imitates an instinctive mannerism without simultaneously and spontaneously experiencing the antecedent feeling.

But acting (intentional imitation of instinctive mannerisms) is different
from intentional behavior that may appear to contradict the desire
associated with an emotion that the subject actually feels. In the case of
courage, one experiences fear based on an interpretation of present
danger, and while the emotion carries the desire to flee and avoid
the danger, for one reason or another one may reason that attempting
to flee will lead to an even worse outcome and therefore that attacking
is a better way to deal with the danger. In this situation, one experiences a desire to flee the danger, but other aspects of the present
circumstances suggest better strategies and, in the final result, to attack
maximally implements the totality of the hierarchy of strategic desires.

What this example illustrates clearly is that intentional behavior does
not reliably indicate internal experience to a third-party observer, and
that in any particular circumstance the internal experience may be the
opposite of what an observer might infer. In any event, one is "courageous" when one experiences fear but attacks based on an intellectual
interpretation that attacking is the best way of dealing with the danger
— i.e., having the courage of one's convictions. Similarly, one exhibits
"honor" when one experiences shame but, rather than hiding, one
behaves forthrightly based on an interpretation that facing up to and
openly admitting the failure is the best way to deal with the situation.

One who is characteristically able to deal with one's shame honorably
is said to have "dignity." The word "honor" has another usage, as in
"honor bestowed." Such honors give rise to memories of accomplish-
ments with a legitimate basis for evoking pride and which can, when
one feels shame, be recalled to assist one to feel proud. A great inventory of such honors is called "nobility." Behavior intended fraudulently
to deny a personal failure is called "hypocrisy."

CONCLUSION

Chapter One and this chapter have described a model of mentality that can serve to analyze any flow of experiences into irreducible elements. From the perspective of a member of the audience at a movie, it is rarely helpful to analyze the flow of visual images into the irreducible visual elements of the movie (the individual still pictures). Such fine-grained analysis is usually unnecessary (and may be counterproductive) to derive full literary value in the enjoyment of the movie. Even though one may recognize, in principle, that the movie is constituted *inter alia* from a sequence of individual visual elements, it is much better for the literary appreciation of the movie for one to identify (conceive) fictional (fantastic) characters from aggregates of individual elements and to experience vicariously the emotions of the characters (the emotions that one experiences while imagining oneself in the circumstances of those characters). Similarly, most psychological analysis is not helped by a fine-grained analysis of events into individual units of mentation; even rarer is it helpful to analyze individual units into individual constituent experiences.

Most psychological analysis involves the identification of psychological themes that are composed of aggregates of concepts that are experienced repeatedly over long periods involving countless units of mentation — psychological themes such as "oneself," "physical reality," and "other people." Characteristically, these conceptual themes do not change from unit to unit. The themes are the usual elements of psychological analysis in the same way that fictional characters in literature are the usual elements of literary analysis. For literary analysis, it is rarely necessary to analyze literary themes into their elements (individual words or still pictures), and for psychological analysis, it is rarely necessary to analyze the persistent, conceptual, psychological themes into their elements, unit by unit. The themes have developed over a long time-frame, and the psychological analysis usually does not (and need not) analyze the psychological themes into their elemental constituents. Rather, a coarse-grained analysis of psychological events in terms of the themes, but no further, is sufficient. I contend that in the rare circumstance where the themes themselves need to be analyzed into their elements, the fine-grained capability of the elemental model of mentality provides the proper basis of such an analysis.

Even where coarse-grained analysis into psychological themes is sufficient, psychological analysis requires that the elemental characteristics of the emotions that are experienced in relation to the themes be recognized. The elemental constituents that comprise the themes may be concealed, but even coarse-grained psychological analysis necessarily deals directly with emotions that are themselves fine-grained elements. For psychological analysis, the fine-grained aspects of mentation are rarely important, but it is always essential to understand the elemental characteristics of the emotions that are experienced.

In addition to psychological analysis, the elemental model of mentality provides the foundation of a grand philosophy according to which anything can be analyzed. A grand philosophy is a description of the structure of all knowledge — the principles according to which any concept is logically related to any other. The philosophy of elementalism is addressed in the next part.

PART TWO

THE
PHILOSOPHY
OF
ELEMENTALISM

CHAPTER THREE

THE STRUCTURE
OF
REALITY

PHILOSOPHICAL FOUNDATION:
PRESENT MENTAL EXPERIENCES

THE foundation of the philosophy of elementalism is the undeniably self-evident reality of one's present mental experiences. One cannot doubt that one is experiencing a subjective mental experience at the time that one experiences it. If one should want or try to doubt present experience, the wanting or trying would itself be a present experience. Were proof of the reality of a mental experience necessary, the experience of the experience proves the experience.

The totality of mental experiences that one is experiencing constitutes undeniable present reality. Nothing else is self-evident, or self-defining, or undeniable. Not only is nothing else self-evident and undeniable, but there may be nothing other than one's present subjective mental experiences. One experiences nothing else. Anything that one might consider to be something else can be shown by analysis to be a composite of one's present experiences; for example, what one refers to by the terms "external" or "actual" or "objective" physical reality is composed of one's present external sensory experiences and one's present concept of what those experiences signify. Consequently, present experiences constitute not just one's philosophical starting point but also one's end point and every point in between — philosophical reality.

> *Compare two philosophical starting points: the undeniable reality of present mental experiences and* cogito ergo sum. *A philosophical foundation must be self-defining and elemental. If it is a composite of other, more elementary constituents, then the latter are better foundations. Are the elements of* cogito ergo sum *("I," "think," "therefore," "am," as well as the punctuation and syntax) self-defining and simple, or are they composites? "I," "therefore," and "am" are composite concepts. It is my view that when Descartes used the term "cogito" (ignoring the subject "I" included in* cogito*), he referred not only to abstract thoughts but to any mental experiences. Consequently, Descartes correctly recognized, within* cogito, *a core of self-evident elementality. However, in my view, his inclusion of "I," "therefore," and "am," as philosophical foundations was a mistake.*

The challenge of philosophy is not to identify something antecedent or exterior to one's mental experiences, but to understand them. Understanding can take place only in terms of concepts that are also mental experiences. One cannot escape from the philosophical universe of one's mental experiences. This implies nothing about what may or may not lie outside the universe of present mental experiences, only that it is useless to speculate because speculation could also exist only in the form of concepts and one would not have escaped one's experiences. There may be an objective reality that corresponds precisely with one's concepts (one can never know), but that "reality" has no presence in one's real elemental universe.

There are concepts of exterior, objective reality and of other people with their own experiences. However, the concepts exist as part of the larger all-inclusive universe of one's mental experiences. Since the contents of the concepts derive from other subjective experiences, any reference to something external to subjective experience is philosophically speculative and gratuitous. Mental experiences are self-evident and undeniable and therefore philosophically self-supporting. Present mental experiences need no antecedent. They are, therefore, the foundation, the reality, on which philosophy must stand.

Throughout this book, I have tried to be careful to use the pronoun "one," and to refer to mental experiences as one's own. My usage of the pronoun "one," however, differs somewhat from the common practice. The conventions of polite, civilized communication (for example, between writer and reader) include, as tacit underlying presumptions, what are described below as "concepts of practical reality." Once one has adopted these presumptions, one has assumed what I call the "practical perspective." From the practical perspective, the term "one" is a general pronoun that refers to communicator, communicatee, or anyone else but no one in particular. The terms "one's mental experiences" and "one's own mental experiences" imply that one is the subject/proprietor/creator of one's own private mental experiences and suggest that other people have their own private mental experiences.

In comparison with these practical presumptions, the model of mentality described here implies, first, that one's elemental mental experiences are the elements from which everything (what one calls "the universe") is constituted; second, that everything is potentially capable of analysis into one's elemental experiences; and, third, that one does not fully understand anything unless one analyzes it into its elementary constituents, which are one's elemental mental experiences. I call the posture from which one recognizes these elemental principles the "elemental perspective."

The common usage (from the practical perspective) of the terms "one," "one's own," "one's experiences," and "one's own experiences" suggests that one is the antecedent subject/creator/proprietor of those experiences. However, from the elemental perspective, the concepts "one," "one's own," "one's experiences," and "one's own experiences" are themselves experiences. They are conceptual or intellectual experiences that derive from other experiences, as described above in Chapter One. This implies that one is not the antecedent subject/creator/proprietor of the experiences; rather, the experiences are the antecedent elements from which "oneself" (what one identifies as "oneself") is composed. From the elemental perspective, communicator and communicatee do not have separate elemental existences, nor does a subjective "self" have a separate existence within an "objective" universe. The only things that might, with philosophical rigor, be said to exist are elemental experiences, which make up "communicator," "communicatee," "self," "existence," and everything else. Within elementalism, one can identify nothing with an existence independent from the elemental experiences that constitute it.

Nevertheless, this book must necessarily employ the tools of normal, everyday communication, which include the practical conventions. Those conventions make difficult the articulation and comprehension of the elemental principles that underlie the practical presumptions and that may initially appear to contradict them. It is the underlying principles that I contend are genuine philosophical foundations and that I seek to articulate. Consequently, when I use the pronoun "one" or the term "self," I invite the reader to assume the elemental perspective — to consider that the conventional practical presumption (of an objective physical reality that includes reader and writer, each with an equivalent mentality) is not a philosophical absolute but is only a hypothesis that exists as an intellectual experience within an elemental universe that includes the reader's self-concept.

In reading this book, the reader is requested to treat the "validity," "truth," or "certainty" of conventional practical presumptions as open philosophical questions that this book addresses below. I use the pronoun "one" because it seems neutral. It seems to carry less practical baggage than any alternative, but the usage in this book seeks to remove even that baggage. The pronoun "one" in this book does not refer to anyone as an elemental philosophical entity. I use it, rather, as a broad, unifying conceptual theme (in the nature of a literary device) within the universe of present experiences. When I use the term "one's experience," I do not mean to suggest that there is an antecedent person (oneself) who experiences the experience. On the contrary, experiences are the antecedents of what one identifies as oneself.

In practical circumstances (see below, Natural Concepts of Practical Reality), one adopts the practical hypothesis of an external physical reality, including other people with their own private mental experiences, despite the philosophical leaps involved. The practical world of "actual" or "objective" reality is more properly described as philosophically "virtual."

> *The existence of an external physical reality is not a proper philosophical starting point but is only the content of an intellectual experience that is only part of the larger reality of all of one's present mental experiences. In the diagrammatic representation of mentality described in Chapter Two above, an arrangement of monitors in a circle represents the elemental universe. The circle is divided into segments, and the monitors in each segment represent a type of elemental experience (for example, the external sensory segment contains seven monitors; the emotional segment, twenty-two; and the intellectual segment, only one, which displays the content of currently experienced concepts). The total content of the images on all the monitors within the present unit of mentation represents undeniable reality — the universe. Only the intellectual monitor represents present concepts. Concepts are represented by only one monitor of many, and only it may contain the concept of "external physical reality." The experience of the concept of an external physical reality (or any other concept) is only part of the larger, undeniable reality of all present experiences, but (as with all concepts) its content may be "wrong" (see below, Efficacy).*

PHILOSOPHICAL REALITY

Undeniable
In the expression "undeniable present reality," what does "undeniable" mean? To say that one's present experiences constitute undeniable reality is not to say anything about the truth or certainty of any particular proposition. For the moment, put aside precisely what "truth" and "certainty" mean (see below, Validity). Only propositions can embody truth or validity or certainty. Propositions (as with any communication or any string of words, including the previous sentence) contain only intellectual content; they are the content of concepts. Truth, certainty, doubt, and so on exist only as the content of some intellectual experiences, which are themselves only one of the five types of elemental

THE PHILOSOPHY OF ELEMENTALISM

THE PHILOSOPHY OF ELEMENTALISM

experiences that make up undeniable present reality. Were one to doubt the reality of present experiences, the doubt would exist only as part of one's present experiences. One cannot reasonably question the reality of one's present experiences because the questioning would exist only as a part of those experiences — or, put another way, the reality of present experience exists above (logically precedes) certainty or doubt or questioning, which exist only as part of intellectual experiences. Were one to deny present experiences, one would experience the denial as the content of an intellectual experience and the elemental existence of the denial would contradict the content of denial; therefore, the content of the denial would be wrong; therefore, present experiences are undeniable. To me, this line of reasoning has some compelling logical authority, but that does not make it "true" or "valid" (see below, Efficacy).

Present
What is meant by "present" in the term "undeniable present reality"? In the elemental model of mentality, undeniable reality is analogous to a photograph of the present displays on all the monitors, for which the duration of the photographic exposure is the duration of the present unit of mentation. Even though the passage of time is experienced within one unit of mentation (a rhythmic external sensory experience), the totality of sensory and bodily experience occurring within a unit of mentation is conceptualized only once within that unit of mentation, only in stage 2 as a concept of reality; in that sense only, reality is static — a snapshot, not a continuously changing motion picture. The present (static) display on the intellectual monitor contains the present concept of reality that may or may not include the concept of continuous hierarchical time connected to prior and subsequent units. Even if so, however, continuous time would be the content of a present concept. The multi-dimensional concept of reality includes the entire intellectual inventory (most of it in deep background). The universe is self-contained within the present, and that universe contains one's full intellectual inventory.

The detail within the present concept of reality may include temporal and spatial depth and continuously changing reality. But just as the surficial grain of finely polished wood or stone sometimes gives the illusion of depth, the apparent temporal and spatial depth of reality is an illusion in the present deriving from one's present concept of reality. For most practical purposes, the concept of temporal and spatial continuity is efficacious, but for philosophical purposes that concept must be understood to be an undeniable present intellectual experience the content of which could be wrong. (See below, Natural Concept of Practical Reality, for a discussion of the practical/philosophical distinction, and Efficacy for the meaning of "wrong.") Undeniable reality consists of particular present (static) experiences, including perhaps the static concept of a changing reality within temporal and spatial continuity.

Self-defining
This book uses common terms that identify categories of elemental experiences, but it is the experiences that are original and define the terms, not vice versa. Those terms can have meaning only to one who has that type of experience as part of one's constitution. The terms exist only as the content of intellectual experiences that make sense of (logically relate) the original elemental experiences. The intellectual semantic meanings of the terms derive from reference to those original experiences. The elemental experiences precede the terms. The antecedent experiences are the elemental stuff from which intellectual definitions are derived. In that sense, the original experiences are self-defining. On the other hand, the definition of anything else derives from the initial experiences to relate which the definition was created.

Intellectual definition is one thing, but within the model of mentality described here, the real "meaning," or functional significance, of anything derives from its connection to value. Maximizing value (possible only by maximizing experiences with value) is the purpose of life, the function of mentation, and the ultimate standard by which anything is judged (evaluated). The reason one attributes intellectual or semantic meaning to terms is that one conceives that doing so will maximize value.

EFFICACY

"Validity"

Philosophy might be described as the effort to identify concepts that have a particular characteristic — for the moment, call that characteristic "validity." One thinks of philosophical validity as having a kind of universality: a philosophically valid concept is valid always and everywhere. What is the significance of a concept being valid? Can that characteristic be described? How does one determine the validity of a concept? What is the significance of concepts that are not valid? Would a grand catalogue of all philosophically valid concepts demonstrate some kind of coherence? And what of the remaining invalid concepts?

> *The validity of a concept refers only to its content. The experience of a concept, when experienced, is undeniable, but the content of that concept may be valid or invalid.*

Philosophizing (trying to identify philosophically valid concepts) occurs rarely in life, whereas one is always conceiving reality anew and choosing behavior. One is always trying to come up with "correct" concepts — practically correct for here and now as opposed to philosophically valid for all time and everywhere. Is there a fundamental difference between normal life, in which one is always trying to come up with practically correct concepts, and the part of life characterized as philosophical contemplation, in which one seeks to identify philosophically valid concepts? In retrospect (the part of one's present concept of reality that one identifies as memories), one is pleased with some of one's concepts (and calls them "correct" or "right") and regrets others ("incorrect" or "wrong"). What distinguishes the correct from the incorrect? Is practical correctness the same as philosophical validity? Could one create a grand, coherent catalogue that included all of one's practically correct concepts? How would the grand, practically correct catalogue compare with the grand, philosophically valid catalogue?

First, every concept is experienced as a logical solution to a problem posed in the context of mentation, as described above in Chapter Two.

One does not experience concepts except in the context of mentation. The concepts that one experiences are either (1) a concept of reality in stage 2 of a unit of mentation, where the concept is the interpretation of the feelings experienced in stage 1, or (2) a decision about how to behave in stage 4 that chooses one behavior to maximally implement all the behavioral desires experienced in stage 3. There are no special categories of concepts (as, for example, philosophically valid concepts) that are experienced in a pure abstract intellectual environment uncorrupted by the mundane reality of feelings experienced in the other stages of the unit of mentation. Principles of mathematics or philosophy may appear to be pure, self-supporting, abstract structures, but every time one experiences any concept (abstract or otherwise), that experience occurs either in stage 2 or stage 4 of a unit of mentation as a solution to the problem posed in stage 1 or stage 3, respectively. A concept may seem self-supporting, abstract, pure, or isolated, but that is only because, when it is experienced, it is in the foreground of the present concept of reality. However, the rest of the intellectual inventory, including all the logical inter-connections, is not absent and separate. Rather, the remaining intellectual inventory is only comparatively less prominent in the mid-grounds and backgrounds.

Second, the content of a concept is a logical relation between other experiences. Every concept is logical in that respect. The particular logic reflects the problem to which the concept is the solution. There are at least two reasons why the fact that one experiences every concept as a logical solution to a problem does not lead to the conclusion that the concept is valid or correct: one may have chosen the wrong logic, and there may be important factors that one has not considered. Thus, the logicality inherent in every concept (the logicality according to which the concept seems to be the solution to its problem) does not itself imply anything about its validity.

Third, concepts have no value. There is nothing inherent about a concept that identifies whether or not it is valid, even though it is a logical solution to a particular problem.

Fourth, one has no access to a reality independent of one's present experiences (an "actual reality") against which to test the validity of one's concepts. Since the elemental universe is self-contained within present experiences, what one identifies as the validity of a concept must also derive from present experiences. Past experiences cannot measure the validity of a concept, because what one now considers to be past experience is a present concept (a memory) that may itself be invalid. By the same reasoning, future experiences afford no basis to test the validity of a concept, because what one now considers to be the future is also a present concept that may be invalid, and even if one conceives the "future" to have arrived, the test that is now conceived to have been conceived in the past would itself be a present memory that could be invalid. Consequently, one has nothing but present concepts to validate present concepts, and all could be invalid.

What is the significance of "correctness"? The answer to that question derives from the function of concepts. The function of any element of mentality is the function that it serves in mentation. The function of concepts is to translate feelings (external sensory experiences, internal bodily experiences, and emotions) into behavior that maximizes value. Translation takes place by means of the concepts created at the second and fourth stages within each unit of mentation: conceiving reality and choosing behavior. "Choosing behavior" is shorthand for "conceiving the output to activate that will, in consequence of being activated, instantiate behavior to lead to greatest value." Hereafter, a concept will be said to be "adopted" if it serves as a basis for conceiving reality or for choosing behavior — i.e., if it is used to maximize value. To maximize value is the purpose of mentation, in the service of which concepts are formed. Consequently, given a choice of logical concepts, one adopts the concept that one conceives will maximize value. One adopts a concept as a basis for choosing behavior because one currently conceives that it will be efficacious for the purpose of achieving value in the future. That is, one currently conceives that its adoption in the present unit of mentation (now) will lead to maximum value in subsequent units (later).

Hereafter, the special characteristic that philosophers seek in concepts will be called "efficacy in achieving value" (or just "efficacy") rather than validity. (The words "efficiency" or "effectiveness" would do as well.) In this respect, we are all philosophers and correctness is synonymous with validity. At the time of its adoption (now), one knows that a concept is a logical solution to a particular problem, but one does not know whether its adoption will maximize value in the future. Only in the future can the present adoption of a concept be validated or considered correct. By then, one would be in a different unit of mentation in which the adoption of that concept in the past would be a present memory that could be false. A concept cannot be validated by another which itself is not validated.

One considers a particular concept to be efficacious if one determines that the adoption of that concept in the present unit of mentation is one's best choice to maximize value in the future while recognizing that there might be a better choice of which one is unaware.

One often has logical reasons to expect that the adoption of a concept in the present unit of mentation will result in value in subsequent units (one has good reason to be confident in most of one's decisions; see below, Tentativity and Belief), but life demonstrates unequivocally that confidence and reason to expect value in the future are not the same as validity or correctness and are often unpredictably mistaken and forsaken.

What would be contained in the grand catalogue of "valid" or correct concepts? The concept "2" is the logical solution to the problem "Within the natural number system, what is the sum of 1 and 1?" The concept "1 + 1 = 3" might be called an "absurdity" that contradicts the concepts included in the natural number system, but it is a logical solution to the problem "Provide a concept that contradicts 1 + 1 = 2." When faced with the problem of providing a concept that contradicts 1 + 1 = 2, the concept "1 + 1 = 3" would be efficacious.

The example of "1 + 1 = 3" demonstrates that all concepts have some efficacy. In considering the sum of 1 and 1, the concept "1 + 1 = 2" would probably lead to value more often than "1 + 1 = 3"; however, the example illustrates that seemingly absurd concepts can serve to achieve value in specific circumstances. Philosophy, then, cannot simply divide concepts into two discrete groups — the valid and the invalid; the right and the wrong; the efficacious and the inefficacious. Efficacy is not an absolute characteristic of a concept. Rather, a concept may be efficacious in some circumstances and inefficacious in others. What is important is to identify the circumstances in which it is efficacious to adopt a concept. The circumstances in which it is efficacious to adopt a concept are called its "domain of efficacy" or "domain of adoption." Each concept has a domain. However ridiculous or absurd a concept may seem in most practical circumstances, there is some domain (however small) in which adopting the concept will prove efficacious in the quest for value; for example, fantasies may be entertaining.

Since every concept has a domain of efficacy, every concept must be included in the grand catalogue of philosophically valid or practically correct concepts. The coherence of one's understanding of the universe consists not in the identification of the few concepts that are sacrosanct as distinct from the rest that are unclean. Rather, the coherence derives from the organization of all concepts into domains. The grand catalogue then must be organized or structured to include every concept that one has experienced and to identify each with its domain of efficacy. Some of the domains contain others (for example, the domain of the concept of the number system contains the domains of all the individual concepts that make up the number system), but contradictory concepts would have mutually exclusive domains. The grand structure would look like a mosaic of domains, some overlapping, some included in others, and some mutually exclusive. For elementalism, no concept is valid or correct by virtue of its content. Rather, one identifies each concept with a domain within which one has reason to expect that maximum value will result in the future from its adoption now. But since the domain is also conceptual, the efficacy of a concept derives from its position within the organization of all concepts. Even contradictory and apparently ridiculous concepts must be included in the grand catalogue of efficacious concepts, and every concept has a domain within which one has reason to expect that its adoption will maximize value. But a present expectation (even for good logical reasons) is not a philosophical validation with any universality.

No concepts are sacrosanct. All concepts have some domain of efficacy, but inherent in the adoption of any concept is an uncertainty that it might be wrong for the circumstances — the domain might not include the present circumstances. "Validity" cannot be distilled by distinguishing valid concepts from invalid. "Validity" does not inhere in concepts. Rather, the universality that one expects to find in "validity" inheres in logics. If, somehow, one could create a catalogue of logics, one could identify the foundations of "validity" and satisfy one of the objects of philosophy. In the section Intellectual Experiences, in Chapter One, I describe the principles that make up the logic of hierarchies, and in the third part of this book, Elementalism and the Mind/Matter Problem, I describe the principles that make up the logic of causation. But I make no attempt to create a catalogue of logics, and it is not at all clear to me how that task might be approached systematically. One does not experience logics (the principles), one experiences logicality as a quality of every concept, and from similar logicalities one infers principles of particular logics. Principles (which are concepts) can be articulated; logicality, which exists only as a property of concepts, cannot be articulated — it can only be recognized introspectively.

The description of the logic of hierarchies in Chapter Two did not articulate the logicality of the logic of hierarchies, but it provided an example whereby the reader was invited to recognize the logical implications that derive from the definition of hierarchy. The logic is the set of principles by which the definition of hierarchy leads to the implications. The definitions and the implications can be articulated, but one cannot articulate the means by which one determines that the definition leads to (implies) the implications. If the reader did not identify the implications as implied from the definition, then there is no means by which the reader can experience the logicality.

Nor can one validate logic by any absolute or philosophically rigorous means, because logicality would be the means of validation. In this sense, logic is self-validating.

Efficacy
Problems are posed to the intellect in the context of mentation. If one conceives only one logical solution to a problem, that solution will seem to be efficacious — one must recognize that there might be a more efficacious concept of which one is unaware, but one is not faced with a present choice. But if there are numerous logical solutions, then one is forced to choose. How does one identify the most efficacious concept from numerous alternatives when all are logical solutions to the problem posed?

To identify the most efficacious concept from numerous logical alternatives, one considers three comparative criteria: facility, elegance, and profundity. "Facility" is the ease with which a concept can be applied. "Elegance" is the brevity with which it can be articulated. "Profundity" is its breadth — the number of problems for which it is (or leads to) a solution. It may be more efficacious to maintain a small inventory of profound concepts than a large inventory of very specific concepts. However, several specific facile concepts may be more efficacious than one that is profound but clumsy. It is not apparent to me why some elegant concepts are easy to apply while others are very confusing.

> *Common usage of the term "facile" can sometimes contain a disparaging connotation such as "too easy" or "simplistic." As used here, however, the term "facility" refers to beneficent ease of use, and facile means easy to use — not too easy.*

Facility, elegance, and profundity are the three criteria by which one conceives that the adoption of a particular concept, in comparison with other concepts, will or will not maximize value. One applies these three criteria by comparing one concept to the alternatives, not by reference to an external objective reality or to anything external to present experience. Therefore efficacy could be called "internal" efficacy. These three aspects (facility, elegance, profundity) are themselves concepts.

Efficacy is not a matter of relativistic taste, which one can allot capriciously to whatever concept one might want. There is creativity in the creation of concepts, but it is not a whimsical, relativistic freedom to choose whatever concept one might capriciously want. On the contrary, all concepts are rigorously logical in relation to the problem for which the concept is the solution, and one is compelled to adopt as operating hypotheses what one conceives to be the most efficacious concepts (in terms of facility, elegance, and profundity) in comparison with other concepts.

In the practical world of operating a car, the laws of physics governing the mechanics of the car are not efficacious at all because they are not facile enough to enable rapid decisions — it is far more efficacious to remember the unrelated individual functional principles stated in the introduction to this part of the book (that rotating the steering wheel clockwise turns the car to the right, and so on). Automotive engineers consider those unconnected functional principles to be simplistic approximations of underlying mathematical/mechanical principles. For the practical purpose of designing an automobile, the mathematical principles of mechanics are more elegant and profound than any others, and rapidity is not especially important. Therefore, for the purpose of designing cars, the engineer adopts the mathematical/mechanical principles. But the same engineer does not adopt those advanced concepts when he is driving the car, because they are inefficacious for driving, where facility is more important than profundity or elegance. The domain of driving cars is generally distinct from the domain of designing them, and different concepts apply within those separate domains. The borders between these domains adjoin (and perhaps blur) where, for example, an engineer test-drives a car to refine some specific calibration.

One adopts concepts for their efficacy in achieving the particular tasks that one undertakes in order to maximize value. Driving a car requires intellectual speed, but philosophy does not. Philosophy involves profundity, and elegance is valued in philosophy only to the extent that it does not compromise profundity. Therefore the criteria of philosophical efficacy, the criteria by which a concept is judged philosophically valuable, are, primarily, its breadth (its profundity) and, secondarily, the brevity with which it can be articulated (its elegance). If a profound and elegant concept is also facile, that is just icing on the philosophical cake. Ultimately, philosophy is the search for the most concise statement of principles that describe the organization of everything. Whether or not those principles are facile enough to assist in practicalities like driving is philosophically unimportant. To articulate general principles is not the reason philosophers philosophize. Rather, they do what they do for the same reason they (and we) do everything else: because they conceive that that behavior will maximize personal value. For philosophers, maximizing personal value comes through articulating profundities.

Although it is not clear to me why it must be so, it is clear to me that great profundities must have at least two characteristics. First, the most profound concepts state principles by which many others are organized, and thus contained. Second, the organization of concepts contained within a profound concept is coherent, i.e., without internal contradiction.

As to the first characteristic, remember that the profundity of a concept is the number of problems for which the concept is the solution or leads to the solution. Practical problems (for example, deciding how to flee from an attacking lion) often require a solution in one step within the same unit of mentation in which they are posed — for such practical problems, facility governs. But philosophical problems are usually divided into numerous subproblems solvable over numerous units of mentation. A concept that states the principles by which many others are organized contains those others and provides a set of instructions by which to identify one particular solution over a number of units of mentation. Thus, a simple mathematical equation is profound because it contains the solutions to an infinite number of problems. A mathematical equation is a statement of the principles by which all those solutions are organized and contains instructions by which a particular solution can be identified. Of course, the entire corpus of mathematics, which contains an infinite number of equations, is more profound than any one equation. A concept of the organizing principles of many other concepts is necessarily very compositive.

The second characteristic of the most profound concepts is coherence. A conceptual network is logically coherent if none of the constituent concepts contradicts another.

A contradiction consists of two propositions of which one may be stated as "P" (or the logical implications of "P") and the other as "not P" (or the logical implications of "not P"). "Not P" is the contradiction of "P." The relationship between any proposition and its contradiction, between "P" and "not P" (call it the "contradictory" or the "negative" or the "not" relationship) reflects a particular logic that can be recognized in the example presented in the previous sentence but cannot be analyzed into constituents because the logic exists only in the form of the logicality of concepts, only as the property of particular elements, and not as a composite of elemental constituents of its own into which it might be analyzed. The logic of contradictions can only be experienced in the form of the logicality of a concept that constitutes a contradiction.

No proposition contradicts another except in the context of a coherent network of concepts. For example, the natural number system is a coherent network of concepts that are organized according to arithmetic mathematical principles. Within that system, "1 + 1 = 2" contradicts "1 + 1 = 3"; however, within the grammatical system that constitutes the English language, both are grammatically correct and not contradictory. Only in respect to particular organizing principles are two propositions contradictory or coherent; therefore, the complete definition of "P" must include a statement of the organizing principles according to which "not P" contradicts "P."

A logical incoherence (synonymous with discontinuity, or inconsistency, or contradiction) within a body of knowledge implies that the body is composed of separate, mutually incoherent networks. The ultimate profundity would be a statement of principles according to which all one's concepts were coherently interrelated.

Efficacy is not synonymous with truth. The efficacy of any concept has to do with its profundity, elegance, and facility in comparison with other concepts. Truth refers to a correspondence between the meaning (content) of a concept and an "actual" or "objective" reality that is otherwise unrelated to one's subjective experiences. From the elemental perspective, one has no access to, and therefore can know nothing about, an "actual" reality that might, or might not, exist apart from one's present experiences. Therefore one cannot verify the truth of any concept. Philosophically, the distinction between efficacy and truth is fundamental, but for most practical purposes the concepts of an objective reality and of truth are more efficacious than concepts that recognize the inherent impossibility of rigorous philosophical verification. This is because the concept of an actual external reality is, for most practical purposes, more facile than concepts that include doubt about external reality.

Below in this chapter, the natural concepts of practical reality are described. Those concepts have a huge domain within which they are confidently adopted. Absurdities are concepts that seem obviously to contradict the practical concepts and have very small domains that include their use as illustrative of absurdities (for example, 1 + 1 = 3, above) or as fantasies. For practical purposes, the division of most concepts into the practical and the absurd has value, but philosophically such a division is as fallacious as the division into the true and false — not least because practical reality is itself a composite that contains contradictions. The square root of minus one is an example of an absurdity that has a significant practical domain.

Hypotheticality

Hypotheticality is the opposite of certainty. The efficacy of any particular concept in the present circumstance is always doubtful. One cannot doubt that one is experiencing a concept at the time that one experiences it. One cannot be certain, however, that the content of any particular concept offers the most efficacious basis for choosing behavior in present circumstances. The adoption of every concept includes the following inherent uncertainty: there might be a second concept of which one is unaware that is more efficacious for the particular problem one presently faces. This point deserves emphasis. The content of a concept is a logical solution to a problem posed in the context of mentation, and all aspects of the concept are undeniably part of reality when the concept is experienced. Philosophical uncertainty, however, inheres in the adoption of a concept in the present for the purpose of achieving value in the future because one cannot be certain now what concept will lead to most value then. This uncertainty precludes the articulation of concepts containing certainty on which to ground an unassailable philosophy.

The foundation of the philosophy of elementalism is not the content of any particular concept (which might be inefficacious — wrong), but the undeniable reality of present experiences, conceptual and otherwise. This foundation does not lead, by compelling implication, to the identification of particular concepts as true or valid. This book postulates a model of mentality (an organization of mental experiences) not by virtue of deduction from the foundation, but rather by recognition of the tacit principles in common use. The model is not deduced from the foundation. Rather, the foundation is suggested by the model. Going backwards from the model of mentality to the foundations of philosophy is analogous to extrapolating the big bang from present physical reality. The philosophical foundation is implied by the model, not vice versa.

It cannot be overemphasized that philosophical certainty and philosophical doubt exist only as the content of concepts and that the efficacy of the adoption of every concept in any particular circumstance is inherently uncertain; however, the experience of a concept is to be distinguished from its content. The experience of a concept (or any other experience) cannot be denied. Rather, all present experiences constitute the reality within which philosophical certainty and doubt exist. Philosophical certainty is distinct from undeniability. Certainty and doubt, being the content of concepts, can be analyzed, evaluated, and so on. The undeniable reality of present experience, however, cannot be analyzed or evaluated but can only be recognized as the reality within which any analysis or evaluation must occur. The reality of present experience cannot be analyzed because the analysis can only occur ex post facto. If one were to try to analyze the reality of present experiences, the analysis could only occur by means of a decision to attempt such an analysis and that decision could be implemented only in the next unit of mentation. By that time, what would be analyzed would be a present concept of past experiences, but the concept might be wrong. The concept would certainly be different from any non-conceptual experiences that the concept purported to represent. One would not be analyzing the reality of present experiences. Rather, one would be analyzing a concept purporting to represent past experiences, conceptual and otherwise, and the analysis itself would be in the form of present concepts.

When one conceives that a concept will maximize value if adopted in the present circumstance, one adopts that concept and the circumstance becomes part of the domain of the concept. If, however, one should subsequently identify a second concept that seems more efficacious, the second will be adopted in place of the first — the domain of the second will expand to include the particular circumstance, while the domain of the first will contract accordingly. In this way, any adopted concept is liable to displacement by a second that is more efficacious. One is continually experiencing new initiating experiences that one tries to understand by means of prior efficacious concepts that explain prior initiating experiences. Prior concepts are always liable to being displaced by new ones that efficaciously relate both the prior experiences and the new ones. No concepts can be known to be absolutely efficacious, and any is liable to displacement by another that is more efficacious for the particular purpose at hand.

The liability to displacement of any previously adopted concept by a more efficacious one implies that the adoption of a concept is properly characterized as hypothetical, or probationary. The adoption of a concept in any particular circumstance includes this inherent hypotheticality.

The displacement of a previously adopted hypothesis commonly occurs when a new experience cannot be explained by the concepts that explain past experiences, and so a new concept is created that makes sense of both the prior experiences and the new one. Successfully applied, the scientific method of experimental testing of predictions based on a hypothesis serves to create a

body of new experiences that (one hopes) the hypothesis predicts. The prac-
tical efficacy of scientific method cannot be overstated, but the scientific
method does not provide a philosophical proof or "objective" validation that
circumvents the inherent hypotheticality in the adoption of every concept.

Tentativity and Belief

Insofar as the efficacy of the adoption of any concept is hypothetical, the
initial adoption of a new concept is characteristically tentative. Initially,
one explores the efficacy of a new concept with caution (the emotional
experience of fear). To the extent that predictions based on the new
concept prove efficacious, the caution gives way to confidence (the
emotional experience of gutsiness). With confidence, one abandons
concerns about the hypothetical efficacy of the concept, and it becomes
a belief: a concept that one adopts without considerations of hypotheticality. One comes to believe in (infers) the correctness of a concept in
particular circumstances following a history of reliable predictions
based on the concept (a history of efficacy).

Even for beliefs, the history of reliable predictions is a present concept
(a memory) that might be wrong. Nevertheless, for everyday, practical
decision-making, it is inefficacious (for reasons of facility) to recognize
the inherent philosophical hypotheticality of the practical concepts that
one adopts (see below, Natural Concept of Practical Reality). Where
philosophical rigor is required, the hypotheticality that inheres in the
adoption of every concept is not displaced by practical efficacy based
on a suggestive history.

The uncertainty that derives from the hypotheticality inherent in the adop-
tion of any concept likewise inheres in the concepts of uncertainty and
hypotheticality as well. One's experiences might be related in an efficacious
logical system that does not involve uncertainty, tentativity, or hypotheti-
cality, which system I can neither conceive nor rule out.

Despite inherent philosophical hypotheticality, (1) the concepts of practical reality (discussed in the next section) and (2) the concepts of
natural arithmetic (discussed in the following indented paragraphs) are

two examples of conceptual edifices in which one has such great confidence that all tentativity is efficaciously abandoned in practical circumstances, and they are believed. Confidence in the efficacy of a concept always comes from a history of efficacy (itself, a present concept) and not from the compelling logic of the concept. The logic seems compelling only because of the history. The logic is, of course, logical, but it might be the wrong logic, and there might be important matters that have not been considered.

Consider the natural numbers. One has first-name familiarity with only a very few of them. One develops an understanding of addition by means of many repetitions of the addition tables and the application of those tables in many different situations until one has established a history of intimate familiarity with every single-digit combination, with many double-digit combinations, with fewer triple-digit combinations, with yet fewer quadruple-digit combinations, and so on. At some point, one has identified some general principles of addition, but one does not become confident adding until one has an extensive history of the successful adoption of those principles.

There is a logical connection between addition and subtraction. But having achieved confidence with addition, one is not automatically confident with subtraction merely because of the logical connection between them. Rather, one has to go through the whole process of learning the subtraction tables until one is confident with one's understanding of subtraction. Confidence in adding does not imply confidence in subtracting even though the relation between adding and subtracting is logical. Similarly, confidence in adding and subtracting does not imply confidence in multiplying and dividing. But at some point in one's history, one recognizes that the four arithmetical operations are part of a coherent system that seems to have its own unambiguous organization. One becomes utterly confident that the system can be adopted in any circumstance analogous to commercial transactions involving the sale of bushels of grain, which transactions the arithmetic system was initially developed to facilitate. One efficaciously forgets (1) that each concept in the system is a separate creation that was tentatively adopted until a history of reliable predictions was developed and (2) that one's entire history concerns only a very few of all possible numbers. One's confidence in the arithmetic system extends to such concepts as: the sum of 1 and 1 is not 3, and negative numbers do not have square roots.

To a person confident in the natural number system but unfamiliar with other mathematics, imaginary numbers are absurdities. The concept of i (the imaginary square root of minus one) is not part of, and as a first impression seems to contradict, the natural number system. It can be regarded as an extension to the natural number system, but it is not a number nor is it anything apart from the abstract properties given to it by its clever creators. Those abstract properties do not have any intuitive coherence and were created specifically to circumvent the logic of the natural number system which excludes the square root of minus one. Whereas ordinary numbers can efficaciously represent things in the practical world, there is nothing in the practical world that can be represented by i — perhaps i stands for "inconsistent" or "inconceivable." The mathematician who first created the imaginary numbers must have been very conscious initially of their hypotheticality, and the initial adoptions must have been very tentative. Now, despite the logical gaps, mathematicians and scientists very confidently adopt the concept i in circumstances where a history of reliable predictions has been developed.

In its early development, mathematics was entirely practical. The properties ascribed to numbers derived from the properties of commercial commodities and the numbers represented practical things. To the extent that mathematical elements took on purely abstract properties divorced from anything practical, mathematics became philosophical.

While the hierarchical order of the natural number system implies that, by counting upwards, one will never reach a number that is less than the starting number, one must recognize the possibility that some clever philosopher might conceive of an imaginary hierarchy, an i-hierarchy, in which the concept of an imaginary lower number reached by counting upwards has some small domain of efficacy. I cannot imagine what other properties an i-hierarchy might have, but the logic of hierarchies would not apply.

The simple logical connection between adding and multiplication does not automatically mean that confidence in adding leads to confidence in multiplying. However, the recondite logical connection between natural numbers and imaginary numbers does not rule out confidence in imaginary numbers. In each case, it is the history of efficacy that leads to confidence, not the logic, which is logical, but might be the wrong logic. Confidence is not a concept: confidence is an emotion.

Conclusion

Philosophy is the effort concisely to articulate the most profound concepts. The elemental model of mentality sets out the principles according to which all concepts are elemental experiences the content of which are logically created relationships between other elemental experiences and are organized in domains of adoption for the purpose of maximizing value on the comparative criteria of facility, elegance, and profundity. These principles, according to which all concepts are created and organized, can serve for the analysis of any concept into logical relationships between elemental experiences: the experiences and relationships into which a concept can be analyzed are its structure. The principles of the analysis are the philosophy of elementalism. All concepts, including those that contradict one another in respect of more limited organizing principles, are understandable according to these same principles. Seen as part of this overall structure, every concept is part of a coherent organization of all knowledge. The philosophy of elementalism derives from the character of elemental experiences that are identified and described in Chapters One and Two above. That identification and description are not intended as proof, and there might be a more efficacious taxonomy that I cannot conceive or rule out. But if one adopts the principles of elementalism (in the absence of more profound principles), some philosophical conclusions seem to follow.

The elemental model of mentality does not identify any particular concept or grand conceptual structure as a philosophical foundation that embodies certainty. One's mental capability imposes rigorous logicality on the creation and choice of concepts for adoption, but even so, one is precluded from identifying philosophically final concepts that are not liable to displacement. This is not to impugn logic or logical reasoning or science, nor is it to imply any type of relativism whereby what seems logical is as worthy as what seems illogical. Logic remains one's only means to create concepts from which to choose, and confidence (based on a history of efficacy) is what one calls a "solid foundation." This is only to recognize that logicality and confidence do not displace the inherent philosophical hypotheticality (the uncertainty) of the adoption of every concept.

Elementalism does not identify particular principles according to which one should choose to behave, nor does it identify particular principles according to which the world is best understood. Rather, elementalism analyzes what it means to identify such principles — whatever the principles.

The next section of this chapter describes the natural concepts of practical reality. I consider these concepts to be the universal foundation of mental competence, not because they are implied by elementalism — they are not — but because they are universally adopted. The natural concepts of practical reality serve, within the practical domain, as a philosophical foundation. The practical domain includes what one calls the "objective physical world" with "other people," etc. Those practical concepts are not necessarily implied from the elemental model. They are only one of many possible sets of concepts that one might have developed to understand one's experiences and to maximize value. I cannot conceive of a more efficacious set of concepts to deal with practical reality, but neither can others be ruled out. Elementalism does not describe one best way for everyone to understand the world, nor one best way for everyone to behave. Nor does it suggest in some relativistic way that one approach is as good as another, or that the whole business is too mysterious to understand. Rather, elementalism identifies a small number of irreducible, foundational elements with particular properties that embody the whole range of conceptual possibilities.

The practical concepts described immediately below are efficacious in practical circumstances, but they are not self-supporting. Rather, they stand on an elemental substructure. Were the practical concepts to be displaced by more efficacious concepts, those replacement concepts would likewise stand on an elemental substructure. The elemental substructure stands on the foundation of initiating elemental experiences. That foundation does not itself have a substructure because it is composed of elements that are incapable of analysis. Because all concepts are created and are analyzable according to the principles of elementalism, the profundity of elementalism cannot be exceeded. Of course, one cannot exclude the philosophical possibility that there are concepts that have not been considered here and that would not accord with the principles of elementalism; consequently, elementalism includes the possibility of a different set of more concise principles of greater profundity — a more compelling philosophy.

NATURAL CONCEPT OF PRACTICAL REALITY

The foregoing in this chapter is general. It describes some of the fundamental characteristics of undeniable elemental reality at the elementary level and some of the characteristics of one's concepts of reality, but it does not identify any particular concepts as necessarily efficacious. On the basis of the foregoing, no particular concepts necessarily emerge as the most efficacious — as the concepts one necessarily adopts.

Nevertheless, certain concepts are "natural," in the sense that they are required as part of the specific concepts that are inherent aspects of emotions. Remember that the experience of each emotion depends on the experience of a particular concept. Without the experience of those concepts, one would not experience emotions. A conceptual network that includes all the specific emotional concepts is "natural" in the sense that it embodies the possibility that full emotional potential can be realized. A conceptual network that excludes some emotional concepts would seem unsuited to the emotional potential inherent in the human psyche.

The term "practical" in this book refers to what are considered the common circumstances of life. Practical concepts are very composite multi-dimensional concepts that logically relate vast numbers of experiences. For example, the sophisticated concept of external physical reality

THE STRUCTURE OF REALITY

contains a hierarchical structure of inter-related concepts of increasing compositivity, at the base of which lie initiating external sensory experiences, and at the peak, the laws of physics. The structure that supports a concept is its substructure. The significance of the category of concepts called "practical" is that, in what one conceives to be practical circumstances, it is more efficacious to abandon large parts of the underlying substructure (to relegate that part of the substructure to deep background) than it is to be concerned with it. The part that is abandoned is the most basic part of the structure: the elemental substructure.

> Consider the concept that one is being attacked by a lion. The practical substructure of that concept consists of (1) the interpretation of, inter alia, present visual experiences as reflecting an attacking lion, (2) concepts that there is a physical reality in which one's own body and the bodies of lions exist, (3) concepts of the bad value that an attacking lion can cause one to experience, and these three concepts themselves have a practical substructure. For example, the concept that the visual experience represents a lion is based on one's previous experiences of lions, etc. All those practical concepts, however, have elemental substructures. Before one can interpret the visual experience as representing a lion, one must first have an understanding that visual experiences are a separate category of experiences, i.e., one must first have some understanding of one's mentality, a model of mentality. Furthermore, one also has some understanding of the hypotheticality of the adoption of concepts based on efficacy. The part of the substructure that concerns the model of mentality, philosophical hypotheticality, efficacy, and so on, is the elemental substructure. If one is mentally competent, the elemental substructure of practical concepts is in deep background and has probably never been articulated. Considerations of philosophical hypotheticality interfere with efficacy when facing an attacking lion or when doing almost anything else in practical circumstances. Consequently, it should not be surprising that practical philosophies regard the existence of an objective physical reality as a foundation.

Much better to run, without hesitation, from an attacking lion than to ponder its reality. Except for philosophical contemplation, the efficacy of a concept does not depend on the profundity of its substructure.

It is not clear to me whether the natural concepts that cause emotions are the same as the concepts of practical reality or whether the concepts of practical reality have some additional organizing principle. Certainly, there is great overlap between the natural concepts and the practical ones.

The natural-practical concepts are hereinafter referred to as the "natural concept of practical reality," or just "practical reality." The concept of practical reality is universal in the sense that it is adopted for practical application by all mentally competent people. A person is considered mentally competent (*sui juris*) only to the extent that he adopts the concept of practical reality in practical circumstances. This is the universal minimum requirement of competence, but I can see no philosophical necessity that a mentality with a full complement of properly functioning elements will necessarily adopt the natural and practical concepts.

∞

The natural concept of practical reality has three parts: (1) practical, external, objective, physical reality; (2) practical, internal, subjective (or psychological) reality; and (3) practical social reality. I posit three parts for ease of articulation, since the individual parts are not discretely separate but overlap. Presumably they develop together. The order in which the parts are presented here is not intended to suggest anything about the order of their development or whether one part is logically more fundamental than another.

The basic tenets of this three-part model of practical reality seem to be universally adopted for everyday application, notwithstanding philosophical incompatibilities between the three parts. For example, a belief in an "actual" physical reality obeying the laws of physics independent of one's experiences is logically incompatible with the belief that the physical behavior of one's body is, in some non-physical way, the consequence of one's independent volition for which one is morally responsible. It is the contention of this book that the logical incompatibilities of these three parts (particularly the apparent bifurcation of knowledge into the humanities and the sciences) can be resolved only by analysis of their underlying conceptual structures from the elemental perspective. (See Part Three, Elementalism and the Mind/Matter Problem.)

Practical Physical Reality

Practical physical reality, the first part of the concept of practical reality, contains the ideas that there is an objective physical world that accords with one's intellectual interpretations of one's sensory experiences and that that physical world exists and behaves on its own independently of one's sensory experiences, whether or not one senses it. The concept of an external reality that is independent of one's experiences is the basis of the concept of truth — a correspondence between one's concepts and independent reality.

The laws of physics are entirely practical. From the perspective of scientific objectivity, this independent physical world composed of physical elements is called "objective reality" or "actual reality." Scientists tentatively validate a scientific hypothesis by the scientific method, whereby predictions based on the hypothesis (but not predicted by other prevailing hypotheses) are verified by experiment. Thus it is insufficient for a hypothesis to relate past experiences logically if it does not also predict diverse future experiences. Of course, the hypothesis is considered disproved and is discarded if experimental results do not accord with predictions.

From the elemental perspective, what the scientist calls "past experiences" are present experiences of memories (part of the elemental reality of present experiences). By the time what the scientist previously called "predictions of future experiences" have happened, they too have become ordinary (present) memories that could be wrong, and the hypothesis is still subject to the same uncertainty of adoption as any other concept — the inherent hypotheticality in the adoption of all concepts remains. This is not to impugn scientific method. It remains the most efficacious approach to understanding one's external sensory experiences. (In this respect, we are all scientists.) What scientific method does not do is determine truth, or explore an "actual" physical reality that exists independently of one's mental experiences, or validate concepts by criteria other than elemental efficacy.

Practical physical reality includes the following four concepts: the concepts of space and time, the concept that space and time are hierarchically structured, the concept that within space and time are located different forms of matter, and the concept that some of the behavior in space and time of some of these forms of matter is predictable, according to certain principles. The practical concept of a physical world includes the identification of some minimum number of forms of matter, such as solids and liquids (including one's own physical body) and some minimum number of principles on which to base predictions. There is no precise point at which these minimum numbers are reached for all circumstances, just as there is no precise distinction between mental competence and incompetence.

> *Space differs from time. In time, one is confined to the present ("now"), but the position of the present in relation to other points of time is continually advancing in one direction. In space, one is confined to "here," but "here" can move from any point in space to any other and back again. Time and space, however, are both hierarchical: for all points in space, the more one moves in space away from a point of origin, the greater the amount of space separating the point of origin from the end point; similarly, for all points in time, the more one advances from a starting point in time, the greater the amount of time separating the present from the starting point and the less time separating the present from every point in the future.*

People vary greatly in the degree of sophistication of their understandings of the nature of space and time, in the number of different forms of matter they identify, and in the principles according to which they predict behavior of those forms of matter. Those variations are not part of the underlying, universal, natural, four-part concept of practical physical reality described above. Rather, they are individual peculiarities that overlie the minimum basic natural concept of physical reality. At all degrees of sophistication (whatever the peculiar individual overlay), knowledge of the behavior of matter remains divided into numerous unconnected sections (modules or islands), each with its own set of principles. These islands represent the domains of different concepts. Furthermore, predictions concerning much of the behavior of matter observable at the human scale are inconsistent and imprecise in comparison with the scale of the physical constituents. Nevertheless, that degree of consistency and precision is sufficient to afford some degree of confidence in many of one's choices of behavior.

The theoretical universal simplicities that underlie the scientific understanding of the physical world are properly regarded as gossamer threads that connect the separate islands only theoretically. For example, solid matter behaves according to one set of rules, and liquid matter, according to a separate, different set. Knowing one set does not lead to knowing the other. One conceives them separately, from separate external sensory experiences. Both sets of rules are, in principle, understandable as the behavior of elementary physical matter and hence as merely different manifestations of one underlying set of rules (the laws of physics). However, when one deals with solids and liquids in the practical world outside of a physics lab, one continues to adopt the separate rules that one conceived before one conceived the laws of physics. The development of the laws of physics necessarily succeeded the conception of the separate rules.

Practical knowledge is divided into separate islands partly because the separate rules are more facile (easier to use and therefore more efficacious in choosing behavior quickly) than the more theoretically profound but clumsy laws of physics. Even where speed is not a concern, there are great gaps in scientific theory. For example, the current scientific understanding of physical elements does not lead to the current understanding of chemistry, and the understanding of chemistry does not lead to the understanding of biology. At present, physics, chemistry, and biology are separate islands that are only theoretically connected. The idea that the properties of physical elements give rise to the properties of chemicals, and those of chemicals give rise to those of biology, is a conjecture — an understandable conjecture but still largely unexplored territory. Furthermore, physics, chemistry, and biology are themselves composed of islands.

The term "conjecture" connotes hypotheticality, but hypotheticality inheres in the adoption of any concept. There is a distinction between the hypotheticality that inheres in the adoption of any concept and the hypotheticality connoted by the term "conjecture." Inherent hypotheticality is philosophically inescapable, but in practical circumstances, a history of efficacy engenders confidence that displaces tentativity, and philosophical hypotheticality recedes to deep background. By contrast, the tentativity associated with conjectural hypotheticality cannot be displaced because a conjecture is precisely a hypothesis without a history of efficacy. A concept that starts as a conjecture ceases to be conjectural once a history of efficacy occurs.

Science cannot at present yield precise predictions of human-scale aggregates of elementary physical phenomena and may never do so. In this sense, the scientific understanding of physical elements remains theoretical and is efficacious only in very specific, unusual circumstances, such as answering questions on a physics test or conducting particle research. But even then it is useless to that part of the decision-making process whereby one moves one's physical body to manipulate the physical pen on the physical paper, which is the practical, physical part of how one answers tests or conducts research.

The theoretical threads that connect the separate conceptual islands of practical physical reality are not substantial enough to afford any practical communication between the separate islands. Despite their tremendous value, the mathematical laws of physics that identify and describe the behavior of physical elements do not afford a basis for understanding most of the behavior of physical phenomena at the human scale. Furthermore, one cannot develop a scientific understanding of the physical elements without first adopting the concept of practical physical reality. Furthermore, one cannot conceive the practical concepts without first having some minimal understanding of the elements of mentality outlined in this book — the philosophical starting point for philosophers, scientists, and children. In this respect, we are all philosophers, scientists, and children. (See below, Practical Reality and Elemental Reality.)

Some of the particular forms of matter that are necessarily included in the natural concept of practical physical reality are inanimate solids and liquids and animated bodies, including one's own. In some respects (for example, when falling off a cliff) animated forms of matter behave in a manner that conforms entirely with the principles that also apply to inanimate solids of a similar physical character. In other respects, however, the behavior of one's own body is best understood only as a consequence of one's decisions directing its physical behavior, and the behavior of other persons' bodies is best understood as a consequence of individual decisions of their own. Call this type of behavior "volitional."

The practical understanding of the volitional behavior of one's own body is part of the second branch of the natural concept of practical reality: practical internal, subjective reality. The practical understanding of the volitional behavior of other people's bodies is part of the third branch: practical social reality.

Practical Internal Reality
Internal reality is the second part of the natural concept of practical reality. It includes the concepts that identify the types of mental experiences and their significance, the concept that one's mental experiences differ from physical phenomena but have a physical location within one's physical body, and the concept that there are specific relations between particular physical phenomena and particular mental experiences. Mental competence presumes the ability to identify some minimum number of different types of mental experiences and of specific relations between physical phenomena and mental experiences. For example, competence requires an understanding that one's volition causes the volitional physical behavior of one's body but does not require the ability to articulate the principles of movement physiology or the mind/matter problem.

While practical mental competence requires the identification of some minimum number of one's mental experiences, that identification does not necessarily include any ability to articulate the identification of those experiences, much less any coherent abstract model of mentality. For example, in practical circumstances, it is essential for one to distinguish one auditory experience (a sound) from another and also from visual experiences, to recognize the similarity between a present sound and a similar previous one, and to recognize the circumstances in which the previous sound was experienced. One can cope perfectly well, however, without being able to articulate in any abstract way how the category of auditory experiences relates to one's other categories of experiences within a larger, coherent, abstract model of mentality.

Nevertheless, it is very curious that a coherent, abstract model of elemental mentality has not been articulated sooner. There are two likely reasons.

First, mental experiences do not need to be abstractly understood, as they embody their own significance (for example, one does not need to articulate what "badness" is or that shame is bad, because the badness of shame is inherent in the experience that carries the behavioral direction to "hide in shame," whether or not one can articulate that concept abstractly). In most practical circumstances, the function of mentation (to maximize value) is well served without the articulation of the principles that describe mentality.

Second, pondering the elemental substructure that underlies the concept of practical reality introduces an inefficacy in decision-making speed in practical circumstances.

For most individuals, their abstract understanding of their own experiences is unarticulated and incomplete. This book contends that if the gaps in common understanding were filled and the rough edges properly contoured, the model of mentality described here would emerge.

Within the concept of practical reality, one's physical body and one's mental experiences constitute one's "self." Similarly, the physical bodies and mental experiences of other people constitute themselves. This practical definition of oneself is efficacious in what one conceives to be social circumstances. It is essential to distinguish this practical definition from the elemental definition of oneself described above, which is a concept within the universe of present experiences. It is philosophically redundant to describe present experiences as "one's" because there are no other experiences that are not one's own and there is nothing else and no one else. The experiences that comprise the undeniable elemental universe are not the property or product of oneself as opposed to anyone else. Rather, they are the elements from which everything is composed, including what one calls "oneself" and "someone else." The elemental universe is unified. It consists entirely of elemental experiences, including the concept that the experiences are one's own. The circumstances in which this elemental definition of "the universe" is efficacious (the domain of the elemental foundation of philosophy) are very limited, namely, the contemplation of the underlying philosophical basis of understanding. However, the part of the elemental model of mentality that identifies and describes emotions has immediate application for any level of psychological analysis — an enormous domain.

It is the thesis of this book that elementalism unifies all concepts on a logical basis. The practical concept of reality described here (scientific objectivity) involves an unresolvable bifurcation between the sciences and the humanities, between the physical and the mental. In practical circumstances, the bifurcated structure of knowledge is efficacious because of its facility. In the impractical circumstance where philosophical rigor is sought, however, elementalism is more efficacious because of its profundity. The bifurcation disappears when physical and mental phenomena are both recognized to be composed of elemental mental experiences within the all-inclusive, self-organized elemental universe of present mental experiences.

Relation between Practical Physical and Practical Internal Reality

At a minimum, the natural concept of practical internal reality involves the recognition of certain relations between practical physical reality and one's mental experiences — particularly that one's external sensory experiences are caused by direct contact between one's physical body and the rest of the physical world and that the intentional physical behavior of one's body is caused by one's mental volition. Furthermore, one's volition is unfettered — what is called "free will." For a discussion of causation, see Part Three of this book, Elementalism and the Mind/Matter Problem, Chapter Five.

The practical concept of internal reality includes a minimal understanding of the different types of mental experiences. Within that
minimal understanding, volition exists as a vaguely defined type of
mental experience that includes instructions on how to behave, that
includes a desire to behave, and that causes one's body to behave.
Similarly, the meaning of "unfettered" or "free" is also vague within the
minimal understanding. Nevertheless, the understanding of both volition and unfettered is sufficient to support concepts of "personal
responsibility" for one's actions.

*Analyzing "volition" into its elemental elements yields a clear definition
and gives meaning to the term "free will." Volition is the intentional effort
to behave in a particular way (the effort to do what one wants to do) and
is analyzable into the experiences contained in stages 3, 4, and 5 within a
unit of mentation: the hierarchy of strategic emotional desires, the decision
how specifically to implement those desires maximally within present reality,
and the effort to implement the decision. There is intellectual creativity in
the decision, but that creativity is strictly logical. One is compelled to use
one's logic creatively both to define reality and to determine how to do
what one wants. The range of freedom is the range of intellectual creativity
to decide how to do what one wants. The range is limited by logic — one
cannot escape one's logic.*

*But this limitation does not reduce one's freedom. Maximum freedom is
the freedom to do whatever one wants to do: what one has determined is in
one's best interest. One would be less free if one's volition were "freed" of
the compulsion to do what one wanted and instead had some "freer" personality of its own that could sometimes compel one to do something other
than what one wanted. Intellectual creativity may be as purely mechanical
and predetermined as are computers: one is prevented from knowing
because one does not experience the reasoning process, and therefore the
intellect will always seem creatively indeterminate in prospect but rigorously
logical in retrospect. One experiences concepts only when they emerge complete into consciousness, and only then can one recognize ex post facto their
logicality.*

The operation of a bad habit should not be considered an example of voli-tion directing behavior contrary to what one wants, because the abbreviated decision-making that the bad habit represents was developed from repeated decisions to do what one wanted, and habits can be changed by volition.

Purpose and volition are closely related. The purpose to which one directs one's life, in both the short and the long terms, can now be recognized: to get the most out of it, the most value. One's volition is the desire and the effort to do what one wants, but the purpose for which one wants to do what one wants is to maximize value.

Present reality includes the present conceptions of optional futures that depend on one's interim behavior. In considering a particular behavior, one conceives of the future that would result from it and of the significance (value) that that future would imply. Part of the concept of present reality, then, consists of concepts of the different potential futures (including the values) likely to result from different ways of behaving. Those concepts (along with the others defining the present) give rise to the emotions whose behavioral directions one is compelled to implement maximally. The emo-tions generated by the concept of a bad future direct one to avoid that future, while those caused by the idea of a good future motivate one to behave so as to achieve it. To the extent that one tries to achieve goodness and avoid badness in the future by following the strategies desired by present concepts of the future, one is compelled to do what one considers to be best for oneself — that is tantamount to free will, even though one's decisions may be as determined as the mechanical computation of a computer.

Practical Social Reality

The natural concept of social reality includes three-fold recognition of other people: that some of the forms of matter that are similar to one's own physical body embody their own private mental experiences, that the types of mental experiences that other bodies privately experience are similar to one's own in similar situations, and that the behavior of those other physical bodies that is similar to one's own volitional behavior is caused by the private, individual, free volitions contained within those individual bodies operating on principles similar to the operation of one's own volition. The concept that physical bodies similar to one's own contain independent mentalities similar to one's own is the basis of all social relations and social philosophy, including morality and justice.

A social system of morality and justice involves the emotions of shame, hatred, and anger. One experiences shame (guilt) when one intentionally breaches one's standard of civility and causes harm to another, and shame includes the desire to hide in shame. Evil (the intention in another to cause harm to oneself) gives rise to hatred, which includes the desire to exorcise the evil from the other by retribution. One feels shame when committing an immorality, and one feels hatred when one is the intended victim of an evil. (Evils and immoralities are closely related but not identical.) Justice is based on anger, which one experiences when one is the victim of a disrespect, and anger includes the desire to punish the perpetrator to teach him respect and to extract compensation.

A social system of morality and justice requires that some plurality of the members of the society share similar concepts of the proper standards of civility and respect so that they experience shame, hatred, and anger in similar circumstances, and each member can reasonably expect the other members to behave accordingly. Mental competence (proper adoption of the natural concepts of practical reality) implies the recognition that other individuals behave in response to private experiences of their own of a similar type to one's own, including their own creative, indeterminate concepts of reality. Consequently, others with similar mental capabilities may conceive standards of civility or respect that are different from one's own standards and thus may experience emotions different from those one would experience in particular circumstances.

As a result, the practical concepts contain enough latitude that no particular principles of morality or justice emerge as particularly human or natural or necessary or philosophically derivable or determinable or appropriate for all circumstances. The same emotions and natural concepts give rise to the whole range of moral and legal systems that obtain in different societies, and one can only imagine the systems that might have obtained at earlier stages of human social history or might yet develop. This does not imply, in any relativistic sense, that one moral system is as good as any other, but it does imply that different social systems of morality and justice represent continuing social experiments to determine the most effective system for particular circumstances. The success of such social experiments depends not on whether the members of the society are happy with it but on whether their numbers increase.

Conclusion

This completes the description of the natural concepts of practical reality, which is the intellectual minimum that is required for mental competence, for normal communication, for society between persons, for science. The huge majority of decisions that one makes are based on this intellectual minimum. The huge majority of circumstances in which one finds oneself are practical in the sense that it is more efficacious to adopt, without tentativity, these minimum concepts of practical reality than it is to understand them as composed from elemental experiences. In practice, neither the logical contradictions between these practical concepts nor the absence of more philosophically elementary starting points results in any diminution of value. Nevertheless, I can offer no philosophical necessity for knowledge to be organized in this practical form and not in some other equally (or more) efficacious form that I cannot conceive.

PRACTICAL REALITY AND ELEMENTAL REALITY

- What one calls "physical reality" is a composite of present external sensory experiences and the concepts that make sense of those experiences. Before one can make sense of external sensory experiences, one must first conceptually distinguish external sensory experiences from other elemental experiences. The concept that external sensory experiences are a separate category of experiences logically precedes the logical organization of experiences within that category. That is, the concept that external sensory experiences form a separate category of experiences logically precedes a concept of physical reality that organizes the elements within that category.

In this way, one first must have some basic conception of the elemental model of mentality before one can conceive practical reality.
Some minimal concept of elemental reality necessarily underlies
practical concepts of reality, even though that elemental substructure,
for practical application, has been relegated to deep background.
Provided that one recognizes that what one calls "physical reality" is
a superstructure based on an elemental substructure and that the
whole conceptual structure is hypothetical, there is no contradiction
between concepts of practical reality and elementalism. The only
"certainty" is the undeniability of present elemental experiences, of
which all these concepts are just a part.

- In practical circumstances, practical reality efficaciously serves as the
  starting point for the organization of knowledge. In the impractical
  circumstance where philosophical rigor is sought, however, the concepts comprising practical reality must be understood to be very
  composite concepts with an underlying elemental substructure, and
  the proper philosophical starting points are the elements that make
  up the entire structure.

- Practical reality is bifurcated into two distinct, irreconcilable bodies
  of knowledge (the sciences and the humanities), each of which is
  subdivided into numerous separate parts. Elementalism identifies
  the few common elements and the principles according to which the
  elements relate, *inter se*, to form both branches of practical reality.
  Whereas practical reality is bifurcated, elemental reality is unitary
  and therefore more profound.

- An understanding of practical matters (such as social and political
  philosophy, economics, and science) can be based on concepts of
  practical reality, but that understanding will consist of separate
  bodies of knowledge. For example, political philosophy and chemistry are distinct. The understanding of these practical matters can
  provide no understanding of the common elemental substructure
  that underlies them all. In practical circumstances, the elemental
  substructure that underlies practical concepts atrophies, for reasons

of efficacy, into distant background: the facility of the concepts of practical reality makes them more efficacious in most practical circumstances than the profundity of elementalism.

- Neither the concepts of practical reality nor those of elementalism embody any type of philosophical certainty or philosophical truth or philosophical validity. One adopts a concept in a particular circumstance because one conceives that it, in comparison with other concepts, will maximize value. Efficacy in achieving value is the governing principle, not unachievable philosophical certainty. In practical circumstances, the concepts of practical reality are conceived to be efficacious for reasons of facility. In the very few unusual circumstances where rigorous philosophical profundity is sought and facility is secondary (as in philosophical contemplation concerning the relations between physical phenomena and mental experiences), elementalism is more efficacious than practical reality.

Practical reality consists of unconnected and contradictory conceptual islands. The term "islands" usually refers to the part that stands above the surface of the water that isolates them. A complete understanding of islands, however, requires the recognition that all islands are connected by their underwater substructures and, furthermore, that some part of the substructure (simplistically, the physical element at the center of the earth) is common to the structure of all islands. Elemental reality includes both the practical superstructure and the elemental substructure: all aspects of reality (including the apparently separate islands that constitute practical reality) are related to one another by virtue of connected elemental substructures. The totality of substructure and superstructure constitutes one structure within which all elements (even apparently contradictory concepts such as 1 + 1 = 2 and 1 + 1 = 3) are logically organized. The part of the structure that is common to all parts of reality (the center of the universe, through which everything is related to everything else) is the elemental model of mentality.

PART THREE

ELEMENTALISM
AND THE
MIND/MATTER
PROBLEM

CHAPTER FOUR

STATEMENT
OF THE
MIND/MATTER
PROBLEM

T HE Mind/Matter Problem is a general heading that covers numerous issues, some of which have been addressed since the beginning of philosophical reflection while others are recent. In my view, there are two core issues that constitute the mind/matter problem, and all other issues are subsidiary to these two core issues.

The first core issue is popularly styled "the problem of consciousness": how can physical elements organized in the form of a brain constitute, or cause, consciousness?

*This part of this book considers the mind/matter problem in the context of the elemental model of mentality described in Part One, The Elemental Model of Mentality. According to the elemental model, only specific types of mental experiences are elemental — consciousness is not an elemental experience. One infers a "state" of consciousness **when** one experiences an elemental experience. One is said to be conscious when one experiences an elemental experience **for that reason only**, and then one is said to be conscious of the experience. One is never conscious, however, of anything other than elemental experiences. Consciousness has no attributes of its own apart from the elemental experiences from which it is inferred. This part, consequently, addresses the question of how mental experiences might arise from matter, not that of how consciousness might arise. There is a difference,* *but I think that the answer to the former should satisfy anyone who poses the latter.*

The second core issue is to understand how mental experiences might cause physical phenomena (for example, how an intention to behave might cause the behavior of one's body).

This part of the book will address both of these core issues and several subsidiary issues that are described below. For both core issues (physical phenomena causing mental experiences and mental experiences causing physical phenomena), the essential challenge of the mind/matter problem is to articulate the relationship between mental experiences and physical phenomena in a way that explains the part that either plays, if any, in the occurrence of the other and resolves the apparent contradictions and paradoxes that are subsidiary to the core issues.

But why is the relationship between mental experiences and physical brains considered a problem at all? In view of the fundamental gaps in the understanding of both mental experiences and physical brain phenomena (and of causation), why does it seem that causation between brain phenomena and mental experiences is a problem? Why not assume that their relationship will (would) be understandable once (if) complete understandings of both physical phenomena and mental experiences are (were) achieved?

One reason why mind/matter causation seems to be a fundamental problem has to do with causal exhaustivity of the laws of physics and physical determinacy.

One turns to science for an understanding of matter, but science does not speak with one voice. Individual scientists differ in their understandings of particular physical phenomena, and any particular scientist may adopt one theory to describe one class of physical phenomena and another, apparently contradictory, theory to describe a different class. This part of the book contains brief descriptions of aspects of several scientific theories. No such description is intended to be definitive either as a description of present scientific theory or of what scientific theory ought to be. Elementalism has nothing to add to science. All science is practical in the sense that it is based on the concepts of practical reality that are described in Part Two of this book, The Philosophy of Elementalism, and that conceptual foundation underlies all manner of different scientific theories, even contradictory ones. Aspects of some scientific theories are described here because those aspects bear on the current mind/matter debate, but they are described only to relate those aspects to their underlying foundations. Contrary scientific theories could also have been considered. Just as no theory can explain its own foundation, science cannot explain practical reality. Science can only recognize the practical reality on which it is based. But practical reality too has a foundation in the elemental model of mentality. Science has nothing to add to elementalism.

At the present state of science, all physical reality seems to be constituted from a very few types of elementary physical constituents (hereinafter called "physical elements"). The physical elements may be categorized as (1) particular forms of matter, (2) particular forms of energy, (3) time, and (4) space, each with particular, precise properties, and none of the properties involve mental experience. As science advances, the number of physical elements seems continually to be shrinking. For the purposes of this study, it does not matter whether there are four categories, or two, or just one. Furthermore, even though the problem may be called "mind/matter" or "mind/body," it concerns not merely the relationship between mental experiences and physical matter, but between mental experiences and any physical element (for example, between experiences and physical energy or whatever other physical elements science might identify).

Scientists have articulated a very small number of mathematically precise principles that seem to describe an enormous range of relations between physical elements. The classical Newtonian relationships are causal in the sense that they identify a particular physical phenomenon as the unambiguous effect of prior physical phenomena and as the cause of subsequent unambiguous physical phenomena. However, there are other physical phenomena (quantum phenomena, most famously) that are described only in terms of probabilities. Such probabilistic descriptions give reliable and precise predictions over a statistically significant number of occurrences, but for any individual occurrence, a probabilistic description does not predict unambiguous cause and effect. Scientists debate whether God throws dice — whether individual quantum occurrences also reflect unambiguous causes of which scientists are presently ignorant, whether there is causation at all, or whether the probabilistic order reflects some type of causation intermediate between unambiguous causation and no causation. If individual quantum occurrences have unambiguous causes, then the probabilistic description is second best and incomplete. If not, then human-scale phenomena that appear to satisfy definitive, unambiguous causal descriptions may reflect merely very high probability — God may only throw dice. At this stage, there is not the slightest suggestion how an experiment might be designed to identify unambiguous causation of quantum effects and resolve whether God throws dice.

Elementary physical matter consists of quanta that, individually, can only be described probabilistically and therefore ambiguously. Some physical phenomena, however, consisting of aggregates of quanta at the human scale and at temperatures and pressures prevailing on earth (i.e., circumstances not too far removed from those in which people have experiences) can be described with precision according to definitive causal relations without reference to probabilistic quantum concerns — the precision is relative to the scale of the aggregate, not of the constituent quanta. Such aggregates at the human scale seem to exhibit causal exhaustivity. ("Unambiguous" and "definitive," in the context of causation, are synonymous.)

A causally exhaustive system is a regime in which the behavior of the elements of the system depends entirely on unambiguous causal relations between the elements, i.e., where there is no behavior of an element not definitively caused by relations with other elements, and no effects of elements that are not the behavior of other elements.

Some scientists consider that the entire physical world (even at the level of individual quanta) is a causally exhaustive system. That is, they consider that a complete description of any physical cause implies specific, unambiguous physical effects, which implies that the entire course of physical development (everything in the past, present, and future) is fixed, without room for variation. This predetermined physical evolution is called "physical determinacy." At this stage, causal exhaustivity of all physical phenomena and physical determinacy are conjectures that are rejected by other scientists who consider that God throws dice. For them, the probabilistic description of individual quanta is not merely a second best description of an unambiguous reality. Rather, for them the probabilistic description reflects the real character of quanta and, consequently, of aggregates of quanta at all scales. No means to resolve the issue experimentally have been conceived.

The brain is presumed to be composed of the same types of elementary physical constituents obeying the same rules that seem to apply elsewhere. Many brain phenomena, however, remain unexplored, and it is still questionable what principles apply there. At present, it is not known whether brain activity relevant to mental experiences is causally exhaustive, or probabilistic, or without physical cause or order. From the elemental perspective, these three types of order of the physical world (causally exhaustive; without cause; ambiguously causal) are equal philosophical possibilities until one of them is somehow proven. This part of the book, however, addresses physical determinacy more than the other types of order, not because of any philosophical necessity (elementalism has nothing to add to science), but only because much of the current mind/matter debate concerns the contradiction between apparent physical determinacy and apparent mental freedom.

By contrast with the deterministic order that (at least some) matter at the human scale seems to demonstrate, some aspects of "mind" (for example, abstract reasoning) seem to exhibit a genuinely independent volition — a freedom whose consequences are indeterminate. Accordingly, although neither minds nor brains may be fundamentally understood, the understanding is sufficient to identify a freedom of mind that seems fundamentally to contradict the determinacy that may characterize physical brain phenomena.

Scientists think (1) that mental experiences occur only in functioning brains and (2) that brains are composed entirely from physical elements that are governed exclusively by the laws of physics. Taken together, these two ideas suggest that mental experiences are fundamentally physical. If that be true, the laws governing physical brain phenomena also govern mental experiences. But the laws of physics remain silent concerning mental experiences, and, while there may be a hope or expectation of change, there is currently no suggestion as to how the laws of physics might incorporate mental experiences. According to this line of reasoning, no matter how complete and precise becomes the description of the activity of physical elements of the brain, it will be a description of inter-relating physical elements (i.e., forms of matter and energy behaving in time and space), and it will continue to be absolutely silent concerning mental experience. Consequently, mental experiences seem fundamentally physical and yet cannot be incorporated into the description of physical phenomena that the laws of physics are assumed to represent exhaustively. Seen thus, the exhaustivity of the laws of physics is challenged.

Consideration of the second core issue of the mind/matter problem also suggests a problem of exhaustivity. One's mental competence is based on the concept that one's mental experiences control at least some aspects of the behavior of one's body: that those mental experiences characterized as "exertion of effort intending to cause one's body to behave in a particular way" cause the physical events characterized as "the behavior of one's body corresponding to one's intention." But the laws of physics (which govern the physical elements constituting one's body) are thought to admit of no causes of physical events other than physical causes. So by this definition of the problem, mental experiences seem to cause physical effects, and this also seems to contradict the exhaustive nature of the laws of physics. Of course, if the laws of physics are not causally exhaustive, then a mental cause of a physical effect is not a contradiction, and the problem is how to articulate new laws to include more than physical causes.

At this time in the history of science, three avenues seem to be converging: (1) neurosurgery and neuroanatomy, (2) physics insofar as it provides understanding of the precise atomic and subatomic physical phenomena that constitute brain activity, and (3) computer science and artificial intelligence. Some scientists now believe that science will soon reach the stage that the solution to the first core issue may be found. That is, they believe that some mental experiences will soon be understood as the consequence of the behavior of physical elements or, at least, that there will soon be some explanation of how physical elements might be organized so as to result in mental experience. The most enthusiastic scientists contemplate that the mystery of the organization of mental experience will yield to advances in the understanding of brain physics — that the advance of brain physics will articulate the relationship between mental experiences and physical brain phenomena in the form of laws that will clarify the features of mental experience with "scientific precision" and thereby achieve what the discipline of psychology has not.

If mental experiences are fundamentally physical and physics is causally exhaustive, then the laws of physics that completely govern physical brain phenomena also completely govern mental experiences. If this be true, some troubling implications seem to follow. These troubling implications are the subsidiary issues of the mind/matter problem addressed in this part of the book:

- Mental experiences have no function in determining bodily behavior because physical brain/body activity, without volition, determines behavior.

- There would seem to be no evolutionary reason why mental experiences developed in our species, whose evolutionary success derives from appropriate bodily behavior, not from appropriate mental experiences.

- One's mind is not autonomous but is a slave to inanimate, determinate, brute relations between physical elements.

- The whole basis (mental autonomy) of Western morality and legality is fallacious.

By contrast, there are thinkers who consider that science will never be any closer to understanding how mental experiences might be related to physical phenomena in the brain, and that science will never articulate the relations between brain and mind, much less reveal the organizing principles of mental experiences.

For the relationship between mental experiences and physical phenomena to be articulated, both must first be identified with some precision whether by abstract definition or otherwise. This book identifies elemental mental experiences and describes a model of mentality according to which elemental experiences are organized. From that model, an elemental philosophical perspective emerges. Elementalism provides a framework within which some of the characteristics of both mental experiences and physical phenomena can be articulated. Their characteristics lead to some conclusions about the relationship between mental experiences and physical phenomena. Chapter Five defines terms for the analysis of the issues of the mind/matter problem. Chapter Six considers the first core issue of the mind/matter problem (how physical phenomena might constitute or cause mental experiences), while Chapter Seven looks at the second core issue (how mental experiences might cause physical phenomena). Chapter Eight analyzes the subsidiary issues, the troubling implications, and what is called the "hard problem."

CHAPTER FIVE

TERMS DEFINED

T HIS chapter defines six terms that are necessary for discussion of
the mind/matter problem: mental experiences, physical phenomena, hierarchy, causation, understanding, and explanation.

MENTAL EXPERIENCES AND PHYSICAL PHENOMENA

From the elemental perspective, the foundation on which knowledge is
structured is the undeniable reality of present elemental experiences.
The self-evident reality of present experiences is self-supporting and
does not require any philosophical substructure: it does not depend on
the "truth" of any concepts. Concepts are themselves a type of experience. The reality of present experiences implies that no concept can be
verified by reference to "actual" or "objective" reality and, consequently,
that philosophical "truth" (a correspondence between a concept and
actual reality) cannot be identified. Instead of truth, elementalism recognizes efficacy as the basis on which one makes decisions: efficacy in
the quest for value. Efficacy is not determined by reference to anything
"actual." Rather, the efficacy of any particular concept is determined only
in comparison with one's other concepts. This implies, in respect to the
adoption of any particular concept, that there might be another concept
that one has not considered that is more efficacious for the particular
circumstance. (For efficacy, see Chapter Three.) Thus, elementalism

recognizes that any concept might be wrong (less efficacious than another for the present decision), including the concepts that are the foundations of mental competence: the concept of self, and the concept of an objective physical reality that includes other people with their own private mental experiences. Nor can the inherent hypotheticality of the elemental model of mentality be escaped. Nevertheless, for the purpose of considering mind/matter issues, what follows speaks from the elemental perspective. This perspective analyzes everything into the elemental experiences of which it is composed. The basis of the analysis — the principles according to which the analysis proceeds — is the elemental model of mentality, which the reader is invited to adopt for the purpose of the analysis while recognizing its inherent hypotheticality.

Consequently, when terms such as "one," "oneself," "physical phenomena," "another person," "another person's thoughts" appear here, the reader should understand that those terms are not intended to imply that there are actual physical phenomena, actual other people with their own thoughts, and so on. Those terms refer to concepts that exist only as experiences. Furthermore, since the content of any concept is a logical relationship between other experiences, each concept (including concepts such as "actual physical reality" and "oneself") are understandable only by reference to the original experiences that the concept relates. When reading this part of the book, the reader is invited to put out of mind the idea that there is someone else in an actual physical world (the writer) speaking the words to the reader. The reader is invited instead to treat the words purely as the reader's own intellectual experiences and to abandon (only for the purpose of this philosophical contemplation) the idea that the reader has any physical or other characteristics other than the reader's present experiences.

When this book speaks of physical phenomena, it does not refer to something that "actually" occurs in an "actual" physical world that exists whether or not one experiences it (such a world may or may not exist, but one can never know). Rather, it refers to what one's reference to an external physical reality can only refer to: (1) one's intellectual interpretations of (2) one's external sensory experiences, both of which are types of mental experiences. In the aggregate, those interpretations constitute one's model of external reality.

> *Consider any particular physical phenomenon. Whatever one might identify as a particular physical phenomenon, the identification is constituted of particular external sensory experiences and concepts that interpret those sensory experiences to be the physical phenomenon. There is nothing more to that particular physical phenomenon than those experiences that identify it. The physical phenomenon has no properties other than the attributes of the particular external sensory experiences and concepts that constitute its identification, no property of "actuality" or independence from those experiences. What holds for any particular physical phenomenon holds for the aggregate of them all: one's model of physical reality. It is a philosophical leap to consider that there is anything other than experiences. This leap has essential practical efficacy, but for philosophical efficacy, one must leap back.*

One's model of external physical reality is a tentative hypothesis in which one has confidence to the extent that its adoption has led to value in the past. (Of course, one's present concept of what led to value in the past is, itself, a present experience that implies nothing about value "actually" having been experienced in the past. There might not "actually" have been a past.) One has great confidence in some aspects of one's model of external reality; about other areas, one retains serious tentativity; about yet others, one must acknowledge great ignorance. The term "physical phenomena" refers to a complex conceptual edifice that makes sense of sensory experiences, and this conceptual edifice exists only as a composite of elemental experiences whether or not there is an "actual" corresponding physical reality.

When this book refers to mental experiences, it refers to the self-evident experiences that form undeniable, elemental reality. Part of the reality of one's experiences is the set of concepts according to which one organizes all one's experiences. The set of concepts by which one organizes all one's elemental experiences is one's model of mentality, but since everything is analyzable into elemental experiences, the model of mentality contains the rules of organization of everything. Specifically, the experiences of which the grand model of mentality makes sense include external sensory experiences, which give rise to the model of external reality. Therefore, included in the conceptual organization of all experiences is the model of external reality (including the laws of physics and, perhaps, the concept that external reality actually exists independently of one's subjective experience).

The mind/matter problem may be stated thus: Is there a contradiction between one's model of physical reality and one's model of mentality? From the elemental perspective, however, the mind/matter problem may be stated thus: Is one part of the organization of the all-inclusive universe of present mental experiences (the concept of autonomous, indeterminate, subjective aspects of one's mind) consistent with another part (the model of external reality, which includes the exhaustive laws of physics and is determinate)? Or put another way: Is the grand organization of experiences internally consistent? The mind/matter problem is not whether, or how, two separate systems (the mental and the physical) interrelate. There may "actually" be two separate systems, or the mental may "actually" be constituted from the physical, but one is confined to one's mental experiences and can have no knowledge of anything other than elemental experiences. Furthermore, one's experiences are undeniably real. What one might consider to be an independent "actual" reality should be considered "virtual" because it is also constituted from one's experiences and is, in that sense only, real.

It must also be emphasized that framing the problem in terms of one's subjective universe does not avoid the "real" mind/matter problem of how "actual" physical elements cause mental experiences. This "real" problem is itself part of one's subjective universe. One can know nothing about an "actuality" or a "reality" that exists independent of one's experiences, and the attribution of the property of "actuality" to anything is an intellectual leap, a leap that is practically but not philosophically warranted. Nothing in "scientific method," "pure reasoning," or "objective reality" affords a philosophical escape from one's subjective universe into someplace "actual." The invaluable concepts of "scientific method," "pure reasoning," and "objective reality" derive their power from their efficacy within one's conceptual model of the universe of one's experiences rather than from some genuinely objective attributes (whatever that might mean). The problem defined in elemental terms is the real problem.

To summarize the definitions of mental experiences and physical phenomena: The term "mental experiences" refers to the types of elemental experiences identified in Part One of this book, The Elemental Model of Mentality. Elemental experiences are not composed of constituents and cannot be defined in other terms because any terms by which one might try to define them would themselves be composed of elemental experiences. Elemental experiences are self-defining. The experiences define the names given to the experiences, not vice versa. Elemental experiences can be identified only introspectively and then given the arbitrary names that now appear in dictionaries. What one calls "physical phenomena" can now be defined as those phenomena constituted of (1) one's external sensory experiences and (2) the concepts that one has created to make sense of external sensory experiences. External sensory experiences and concepts making sense of them are the elemental experiences from which what one calls "physical phenomena" are constituted.

It is essential to distinguish between, on the one hand, (1) what one identifies as physical phenomena, which are defined by (a) one's external sensory experiences and (b) one's conceptual model of external reality, and, on the other hand, (2) an "actual" external reality that includes "actual" physical phenomena that exist independently of one's mental experiences. One experiences only one's subjective mental experiences and the types of one's experiences are precisely identified; one does not experience "actual" reality. One experiences one's external sensory experiences, from which one creates a conceptual model (itself a mental experience) of an external reality. That conceptual model may include the hypothesis of an "actual" physical reality that exists independent of one's experiences and that causes and corresponds with one's experiences (call that the "hypothesis of actual physical reality" or the "actual hypothesis"). A hypothesis of actual physical reality is philosophically gratuitous but understandable as a matter of efficacy in *practical circumstances where facility is more important than philosophical rigor. If the property of actuality were neatly excised from one's concept of physical reality, what would remain would be exactly the same conceptual structure, changed only by the qualifications that (1) its domain would be limited to practical matters and (2) it would exclude the practical philosophical foundation that tacitly underlies practical reality. (See Practical Reality, Chapter Three.) The practical structure that would remain would include the entire history of one's individual sensory experiences, most of which one has forgotten. One's conceptual model of physical reality (the remaining superstructure) would have exactly the same applicability were one to recognize, during philosophical reflection, that "actual reality" might be fundamentally different.*

This is not to deny the existence of an "actual" physical reality that corresponds to one's concepts. On the contrary, one is prevented from knowing anything that one does not experience, including that it does not exist. Nor is this to suggest that one model of external reality is as good as any other, nor that one has any type of whimsical or relativistic freedom in one's choice of models. On the contrary, one has creative intellectual freedom, but the range of freedom is limited to concepts that make rigorous logical sense. One's concept of external reality is the result of having applied one's logic to the problem of relating all one's external sensory experiences. One's inescapable elemental perspective requires that one understand "actual physical reality" to be part of the elemental universe composed of elemental mental experiences, not vice versa. Whether or not there is an actual physical reality that is independent of one's experiences, what one refers to as "physical reality" or as "actual physical reality" is constituted from (1) external sensory experiences and (2) concepts relating external sensory experiences, all of which are elemental mental experiences.

The point cannot be overemphasized. What follows defines physical phenomena as phenomena that are constituted of physical elements, which in turn are constituted of one's external sensory experiences and one's concepts. This definition, however, refers not to "actual" physical elements that "actually" correspond to one's experiences in some unverifiable way. The question here is not whether a tree falling in the woods makes a noise if no one is there to hear it, but whether the falling tree makes a noise if one conceives that one is there in the forest and does hear it: i.e., if one experiences visual and auditory experiences that one interprets as a tree falling in the woods, is there an "actual" reality that corresponds to that interpretation? About "actual" phenomena one can know nothing, but about one's external sensory experiences and concepts, one can proceed logically.

HIERARCHY

Hierarchies concern order and magnitude. The concepts of order, magnitude, and hierarchy derive from logics that inhere in one's intellect. (See Intellectual Experiences, Chapter One.) Hierarchies are ordered according to increasing or decreasing magnitude. The simplest hierarchy of increasing magnitude is a set of members ordered such that each member has greater magnitude than its immediate predecessor and less magnitude than its immediate successor. From this definition, the logic of hierarchies implies that the magnitude of any member (1) is greater than the magnitude of all predecessors (not just the immediate predecessor) and (2) is less than the magnitude of all successors (not just the immediate successor). These implications cannot be directly proven; they can only be recognized as logical.

A complexity is introduced where some members of a hierarchy have equal magnitude. In such a hierarchy, the members that are equal in magnitude constitute a subset or echelon of which each member is at the same level of magnitude in the hierarchy, and no member of the subset is a predecessor or a successor of the others but each member of the subset is an immediate predecessor to the member of the hierarchy next greater in magnitude and an immediate successor to the member of the hierarchy next lesser in magnitude. In such a hierarchy, each member of such a subset is at the same stage or echelon or level of magnitude in the hierarchy in comparison with the other members of the hierarchy that are at different levels of magnitude.

One cannot, consistent with these definitions, conceive of a hierarchy of increasing magnitude in which the magnitude at each level in the order exceeds the magnitude of the immediately previous level and yet does not exceed all previous levels. Consider, for example, the natural number system. One recognizes that each number represents a magnitude and that the numbers relate to each other in hierarchical order of their magnitude. There is no number in the natural number system where the next larger number would be less than any previous number, but this "no number" cannot be proven, because one cannot consider every number individually — there are too many. Nevertheless, mathematicians acknowledge the elemental logic of hierarchies and accept, without proof, that every succeeding natural number is larger than every predecessor. The implications of order, magnitude, and hierarchy derive from one's inherent logics and cannot themselves be proven. Rather, they serve as the basis of proof for other relationships. There are other relationships in which, say, cyclicality is a characteristic (where the order is such that proceeding through the ordered stages ultimately leads back to the point of beginning), but that ordering would not be hierarchical.

CAUSATION

Consecutive Causation
One aspect of the mind/matter problem concerns the causality or otherwise of the relationship between physical phenomena and mental experiences. The preceding sections describe something of the natures of physical phenomena and mental experiences, but causation is a third element of the problem. The nature of causation therefore must also be understood in order to answer whether there is causation between the physical and the mental.

The term "causation" has two common usages. Every time the term is used in the mind/matter context, it is important to identify which usage is intended. A description of the most common usage, here called "consecutive causation," follows immediately. Wherever the term "causation" appears below, it means consecutive causation, unless I specify the other common usage, "constitutive causation."

The principles on which the intellect creates concepts from mental experiences are the principles of logic that inhere in one's intellect. The logic of causation is a particular logic just as the logic of hierarchies is a particular logic. Causation is the relationship that one recognizes between two phenomena — (1) the "cause" and (2) the "effect" — whereby the cause causes the effect. One's intellect has the inherent capability of recognizing the nature of causal responsibility for which the words "cause" or "is responsible for" or "makes happen" provide mere identification and not definition. The causal relationship reflects an inherent logic that cannot be analyzed into more basic elements.

The simplest conceptual model of an ideal causal relationship involves (1) a phenomenon (C) that is the cause, (2) a phenomenon (E) that is the effect, (3) a point or interval of time (T) following the occurrence of C and preceding the occurrence of E, and (4) causal responsibility of C for E. Call this simplest model an "elementary causal relationship." Causal responsibility, the fourth element of an elementary causal relationship, is the elementary logical relationship that can only be recognized but cannot be explained or analyzed in other terms. To attempt to analyze causal responsibility into more elementary constituents would be a hopeless task because it has no constituents. The more useful approach is to describe the circumstances from which one imputes causation as an explanation for the consecutivity of C and E and the benefit to be derived from that imputation. More important, what are the minimum requirements for causation to be reasonably inferred?

Not all consecutive phenomena are causally related. How does one identify causal responsibility of C for E about T? How does one distinguish causal consecutivity from purely coincidental consecutivity? Might the consecutive phenomena both be effects of a common cause instead of the prior phenomenon being the cause of the subsequent? There are subtle but crucial distinctions between, first, the logic of causation that inheres in one's intellect, second, a particular unambiguous (or definitive) causal relationship between two specific phenomena, and third, the probability of causation between two specific phenomena. Regarding the first, the logic of causation: causation is a particular logical relationship that one's intellect has the inherent ability to impute between one's experiences that cannot be analyzed into constituents. Regarding the second, a particular unambiguous causal relationship in which C definitively causes E: one cannot prove or deduce or otherwise "know" unambiguous or definitive causation in any particular instance. The most that one can infer in any particular instance is the third: probable causation. Probable causation by C of E is suggested by a history of consecutive occurrences of C and E about T, provided that the occurrences of C are indeterminate in time and varied in circumstances. It is the varied and indeterminate occurrences of C that suggest that the consecutive occurrences of E are not mere coincidence or the effect of a common cause of C and E, and therefore that C probably caused E. At a minimum, consecutive occurrences of E following a number of temporally indeterminate occurrences of C allow one to infer probable causation as the explanation of the consecutivity. Call this principle "consecutivity despite indeterminacy."

The distinction between definitive causation and probable causation cannot be overemphasized. The identification of a definitive causal relation between two specific phenomena cannot be achieved, whereas probable causation may reasonably be inferred from minimal consecutivity despite indeterminacy. The inference of probable causation always includes the possibility that the prior pattern of consecutivity is purely coincidental.

Question: How does one identify unambiguous causal responsibility of C for E? Answer: unambiguous causation by C of E cannot be determined, but probable causation (not "causation," but only "probable causation") can be inferred from a history of C preceding E about T where the occurrences of C are known to be temporally indeterminate. In the history of consecutivity, most important are those occurrences of C that one instantiated in consequence of one's own indeterminate volition. The more extensive and consistent and diverse the history, the more probable that causation is an efficacious explanation: the degree of probability can be determined with exquisite precision from the histories of C and E according to principles described by the mathematical field of probability and statistics.

What does indeterminacy mean and how does one identify it in the occurrences of phenomenon C? C is indeterminate if its occurrence cannot be predicted. Probable causation by C of E about T is easiest to infer from a history of occurrences of C preceding E about T where the temporal order of occurrences of C follows a random pattern determined only by one's own indeterminate volition — for example, a history of (E) the sounds of a door buzzer following (C) the depressions of the door buzzer button where the occurrences of the button depressions followed no predictable pattern because the depressions were determined only by one's own indeterminate volition. (For indeterminacy of volition see Personal Responsibility for One's Behavior, in Chapter Seven below.) One infers that each depression of the button probably caused the buzzer sound because the sound followed the same indeterminate pattern as the button depressions. For one to instantiate occurrences of C in an intentionally random pattern is to experimentally investigate the effects of C. The degree of probability derives with mathematical precision from the particulars of the history of consecutivity.

Probable causation always includes the possibility of coincidental consecutivity or common causality. The adoption of a hypothesis of probable causation, therefore, is initially tentative. One tentatively imputes probable causation between two consecutive but otherwise unrelated phenomena. A hypothesis of probable causation in any particular circumstance forms the basis of predictions that one explores with initial caution, or curiosity, or other emotional experiences. To the extent that predictions are confirmed, the degree of probability changes from purely conjectural speculation to increasingly probable, and the tentativity changes from cautious to confident. A history of diverse reliable predictions gives one confidence (an emotional experience) in that hypothesis. With great confidence, one efficaciously forgets that inherent ambiguity remains in the inescapable possibilities of pure coincidence or common causation, and one confidently regards the consecutivity as unambiguously causal, not probably causal. Nevertheless, great confidence reflects "high probability" at best, not proven unambiguous, definitive causation.

The inference that the depression of the button probably caused the buzzer sound does not prove causation (which is of concern only to philosophers). That inference does suggest that the buzzer sound probably would occur consecutively in the future if one were to push the button again. The significance of the ability to infer probable causation is not that it proves unambiguous causation, but that it affords one the basis for making predictions. The most important predictions are those that concern the effect of one's own behavior. The concept of causation is the basis on which one chooses one's behavior with the intention of instantiating phenomena that one expects to cause effects that will be valuable in the future. Consequently, to say "C causes E" is really shorthand for saying that predictions based on that causal explanation probably will be reliable and, consequently, will maximize value. Despite its efficacy in any particular instance, a causal explanation does not prove causation between cause and effect, nor does it prove anything about the cause or the effect. The inference of causation is independent of the nature of the cause or of the effect but derives only from their historical temporal relationship. Even if the phenomena identified as cause and effect are real, there may be no causation between them. Causation is purely an intellectual creation imputed between phenomena that may be unrelated.

Individual inferences of probable causation from histories of indeterminate occurrences of causes preceding consecutive occurrences of effects (in the form of individual elementary causal relationships) are the building blocks from which the most complex networks of causal relations are constructed. Causal networks are constructed from elementary causal relationships connected to one another either vertically or horizontally.

Vertically connected causal relations are illustrated by the terms "after-effects" and "root causes." Vertically connected causal relations form chains of simple causal relationships whereby C causes E1 about T1 and then E1 causes E2 about T2 and then E2 causes E3 about T3, and so on. Any phenomenon along this vertical chain can be said to cause any succeeding phenomenon. Each link in the chain is an elementary causal relationship, and the connection between links is that the effect in one link is the cause in the next.

One is said to be morally responsible for any intended effect in a vertically causal chain when one instantiates a preceding phenomenon in the chain, no matter how many links separate the two phenomena. Intermediate links in a vertical causal chain of phenomena are called "means" (the means by which a phenomenon in a prior link causes a phenomenon in a subsequent). The causation within any particular link, however, is bald in the sense that the cause causes the effect without any means. One infers causation not from the identification of a means of causation, but baldly from the history of consecutivity. Every causal relation can be reduced to irreducible, elementary causal relationships for which one can conceive no means of causation. Anything that might be identified as a means of causation is itself reducible to a cause without means. For example, the force of gravity may be said to be the means whereby one may cause an apple to accelerate in its fall to earth, but the means whereby the force causes the acceleration is not included in the identification of the force as the cause of the acceleration. Furthermore, if one should identify a means whereby the force causes the acceleration, the means whereby that means has that effect remains unknown, *ad infinitum*. Similarly, any vertically causal chain begins with a cause for which one can identify no cause — no ultimate cause. Causation is efficacious despite the absence of ultimate or intermediate causes.

I have referred to consecutivity despite indeterminacy as the minimal basis on which to infer probable causation. Compare this minimal basis with the very elaborate set of principles that scientists develop to explain causation of particular physical phenomena, for example, principles that involve hypothetical forces that cause the behavior of matter. Such principles serve elegantly to predict consecutivities, but they are not principles of causation independent of consecutivity despite indeterminacy. Those principles are efficacious only to the extent that they predict consecutivities. To the extent that they do not, they are discarded. Consequently, the minimal basis for the inference of probable causation is not merely the minimal basis, it is the sole basis. This is not to impugn scientific causal principles, the importance of which cannot be overstated. This is only to emphasize that such scientific principles are not elementary but are ancillary to the underlying principle of consecutivity despite indeterminacy.

Horizontally connected causal relations are illustrated by the term "side effects." Similarly, there are "side causes," which also connect causal relations horizontally. Side effects follow the model C causes E1 and E2 about T. E1 and E2 are equally both effects; neither is primary or secondary, but one effect is characterized as a side effect only because it has less importance to the person making the characterization. C causes E1 and E2 is really two elementary causal relationships (C causes E1 about T, and C causes E2 about T) that are connected by virtue of the cause in one being the cause in the other. Side causes follow the form C1 causes E about T and C2 causes E about T. Where both C1 and C2 need to occur simultaneously before E is the effect, C1 and C2 are said to be mutually necessary causal factors, but they could be mutually alternate causal factors or the relationship could be more complex. Each particular horizontally connected causal factor can be seen to be part of a separate elementary causal relationship in a particular circumstance where the other factors are held constant, for example, (C1) depressing the button and (C2) putting the main power switch in the "on" position cause (E) the buzzer sound. When the main power switch is left in the "on" position, depressing the button in a random pattern will cause a corresponding pattern of buzzer sounds. Similarly, when the buzzer button is held in a depressed position, putting the main power switch "on" in a random pattern will result in a corresponding pattern of buzzer sounds. C1 and C2 cause E about T is thus composed of two elementary causal relationships (C1 causes E about T, and C2 causes E about T) where the connection is that C1 and C2 are mutually necessary or mutually alternative or whatever.

Networks of complex causal relations can be logically analyzed into elementary causal relationships, and elementary causal relationships can be synthesized into complex causal relationships. The following paragraphs illustrate how one first learns elementary relationships from which one constructs complex causal networks.

There is no practical example for which C always follows E. The history of consecutivity is never absolute. When, after a history suggesting probable causation, an anomalous, contradictory example occurs, one does not immediately discard the hypothesis of probable causation. Rather, one seeks to explain the anomaly by redefining C. One redefines C by incorporating into its definition anything anomalous about the particular occurrence of C that did not precede E; for example, the depression of the button causes the buzzer sound when the main power switch is on. C has been redefined as (1) the depression of the button and (2) the main power switch being on. Both are identified as necessary causal factors (or causes), but neither is considered the morally responsible cause because neither intended to cause the effect. As more occurrences of C and E are included in the history, more anomalies occur and more causal factors are identified. Not all causal factors are always necessary, however. For example, the buzzer will sound when the button is depressed if either (1) the main power switch is on or (2) a battery is in place. More occurrences reveal that the battery will participate in causing the buzzer sound only if the battery is charged. As one incorporates more causal factors and side effects and as one identifies more chains of serial consecutive phenomena (C causes E about T1, then E causes E2 about T2, and so on), one creates expanding networks of vertically and horizontally connected causal relationships. At the theoretical limit of network expansion, everything at any particular point in time would be understood to play a causal role in everything in the next (to leave anything out from the preceding point would result in an incomplete causal description of anything in the next point in time), but one never knows everything about any particular point. This theoretical limit is described as causal exhaustivity of the laws of physics.

The buzzer offers a very clear and simple example concerning which even a very young child can infer probable causation and purposefully direct his behavior to explore and enjoy the causal relationship. In the buzzer example, the conceptions of C, E, and T may seem simple but represent an intellectual achievement for a young child. One infers probable causation whenever one recognizes a history of E succeeding an indeterminate C, no matter how simple or complex are C or E or how imprecisely they (and T) are defined. A scientific analysis of the buzzer example would describe the depression of the button and the buzzer sound not as simple individual phenomena but as complex aggregates of numerous physical phenomena at different levels of physical elementariness and T as a long period of time subdivisible into numerous points separating individual causes and effects, all of which in the aggregate constitute the depression of the button and the sound of the buzzer. The scientific explanation of the causal factors operative in the buzzer example includes a network of separate causal relationships between individual physical elements, and each causal relationship in the network is itself an elementary causal relationship. To understand the complex network of causal relations that constitutes the scientific understanding of the buzzer system, however, one must first begin with the initial elementary causal relationship (the depression of the button probably causes the buzzer sound). The causal network is developed to explain anomalies and side effects within the history of one's experiences of buzzer sounds and button depressions, and so on. In this sense, the relationships in the scientific network are subsidiary developmental adjuncts to the initial elementary probable causal relationship. From the scientific perspective, the individual relationships in the network are real, whereas the initial elementary causal description (the depression of the button probably causes the buzzer sound) is a crude approximation of the real elementary relationships. From the elemental perspective, however, the initial concept of probable causation between the depression of the button and the buzzer sound is elementary, whereas the individual causal relations constituting the scientific description are subsidiary developmental adjuncts to the initial elementary relationship that (after one becomes a sophisticated scientist) one characterizes as a crude approximation of reality. All causal relationships, including the grandest complex causal networks, derive from initial elementary causal relationships in which the indeterminacy of the occurrences of the cause has been identified because they followed a random pattern instantiated by one's own indeterminate volition (by one's experimentation).

The distinctions between the three senses of consecutive causation deserve emphasis. The first sense is the logic of causation by which one is capable of recognizing that one phenomenon causes a subsequent phenomenon. This logic inheres in one's intellect and cannot be proven but can be experienced only as the logicality of individual conceptual experiences. The second sense is the recognition that a particular phenomenon is the unambiguous, definitive cause of a subsequent phenomenon. Causal exhaustivity of laws of physics refers to this second sense by which every physical phenomenon is the unambiguous effect of specific prior physical causes and is the unambiguous cause of subsequent physical effects. Concepts of unambiguous causation are efficacious in practical circumstances (science depends largely on them); that efficacy, however, does not derive from the cause definitively causing the effect. Rather, the efficacy reflects one's intellectual capability to creatively impute causation between consecutive, but otherwise unrelated, phenomena. Even if one assumes there is a physical reality with physical phenomena occurring consecutively, the history of consecutivity cannot preclude the possibility of pure coincidence. In any particular instance, the imputation of causation is a pure creation of one's intellect. It is the logic of causation (and not the physical phenomena that one identifies as cause and effect) that embodies the characteristics of causation. The identification of unambiguous causation in any specific case (the second sense of consecutive causation) is philosophically unwarranted. Furthermore, what holds for any particular example holds for all. The most that can be said about any particular example of causation between two consecutive phenomena is the third sense: that the history of consecutivity despite indeterminacy suggests an efficacious basis of predictions that future occurrences of those two phenomena will also demonstrate the same consecutivity, that the relation is probably causal despite the inescapable possibility of purely coincidental consecutivity.

Causal exhaustivity and determinacy of all physical phenomena derive from a concept of unambiguous causation between specific phenomena. Since unambiguous causation can never be identified in any particular example, however, causal exhaustivity and physical determinacy can never be proven and will always remain conjectures. This does not mean that causal exhaustivity and determinacy are not features of the physical world. Science might reach the stage of unlimited predictive capability where predictions based on the laws of physics are validated in every respect, and scientists would reasonably have great confidence in the concept of unambiguous causality. The philosophical possibility of purely coincidental consecutivity, however, would inescapably remain. Any application of one's inherent logic of causation necessarily includes the philosophical possibility of coincidental consecutivity and, therefore, of ambiguity.

> *Compare the ambiguity inherent in the description of the causal relationship between any particular phenomena with the ambiguity in a probabilistic description that does not involve causation. In the buzzer example, the history of consecutivity despite indeterminacy might give rise to such confidence that it is efficacious to forget about the inherent possibility of coincidental consecutivity (to forget about the probable aspect of causation) and to treat the consecutivity as unambiguously causal. In this example, inescapable philosophical ambiguity is inherent in the nature of causation but, for reasons of practical efficacy, the ambiguity may efficaciously atrophy into deep background. By comparison, the probabilistic aspect of the description of a quantum does not arise because of causation, and the ambiguity will never seem to atrophy in the absence of a fundamentally different description. The ambiguity in the description of a quantum is peculiar to that particular description, and the evidence for quanta (had it been different) might have justified a preferable unambiguous description. By contrast, inherent in any causal description is an inescapable philosophical ambiguity. These two examples illustrate two separate sources of ambiguity. Furthermore, where one quantum interacts causally with another, both sources of ambiguity are operative, and the ambiguities are compounded.*

Where the unqualified term "cause" is used, it refers to consecutive causation, as described above. The term "moral causation" has been defined above in this section as a particular subcategory of consecutive causation.

Constitutive (Simultaneous) Causation

Another usage of the term "causation" is what I call "constitutive causation." To use the word "cause" in the constitutive sense is to say that the properties of the constituents of a composite cause the properties of the composite. For example, one might say that the properties of H_2O molecules cause the properties of water. Water is composed from H_2O molecules; therefore, the properties of water are the properties of H_2O molecules. The properties of water are not something different from the properties of H_2O molecules; therefore, to say that the properties of H_2O molecules cause the properties of water is to say that a thing causes itself. A thing, however, is itself. The proposition "a thing causes itself" adds nothing to the proposition "a thing is itself." The usage of causation in the constitutive sense involves no reference to a point of time that is preceded by the cause and succeeded by the effect. Both cause and effect coexist at all points, and therefore the constitutive usage could be called simultaneous causation as opposed to consecutive causation. The constitutive usage of causation is fundamentally different from the consecutive usage.

Because the scale of a composite (like water) is sometimes so far removed from the scale of its constituent elements (H_2O molecules), they may seem to be different phenomena. That is to say, one's experiences of the composite are quite different from one's experiences of its individual constituents. One's initial conception of the composite "water" is later understood to be an imprecise simplistic approximation of an aggregate of particular individual constituents. The simplistic approximation is a different conception from the conception of an aggregate of constituents. Causation in the constitutive sense refers to the principles by which the properties of the constituents explain that one's initial concept of the composite is an approximation: the principles of the constitution of the composite.

The constitutive usage does not involve normal consecutive causation. There is consecutive causation involved in the relations between the constituents whereby the totality of properties of the constituents at any particular point in time causes the totality of properties of the constituents in the next (at no point is there a distinction between the composite and all its constituents), but consecutive causation relating the constituents *inter se* from one point in time to the next is quite different from the relation between the constituents and the approximation that is one's conception of the composite that is not consecutive but continuously simultaneous. In comparison with consecutive causation, which implies nothing about the characteristics of C or E, constitutive causation implies that the constituents are logically constituted in the form of the composite. There may be many different logics that relate constituents to their particular composites (constitutional or compositional logics) that this book does not attempt to describe, but all such constitutional logics are hierarchical.

A composite is anything constituted from more than one element. "Compositive" is intended to be the adjectival form of "composite" in the same way that "elementary" is the adjectival form of "element," and "compositivity" refers to the number of layers by which a composite is constituted from constituents, and those from constituents, and so on. The relationship between elementariness and compositivity, or by a different description, between analysis and synthesis, is hierarchical. Thus a composite can be analyzed in terms of (analyzed into) elementary constituents, which in turn can be analyzed into yet more elementary constituents, and so on, but only until the analysis reaches the stage of ultimately elementary elements (here called "elemental elements"). Conversely, the synthesis of any things results in something that is more compositive than any of the things that were synthesized. One cannot, consistent with the definition of composite and the logic of hierarchies, conceive that the result of a synthesis might be a constituent element of the things being synthesized. Counting upwards cannot lead to a number that is smaller than the starting number without a logical discontinuity.

When using the term "causation" in the mind/matter context, one must distinguish between the common, consecutive sense and the constitutive sense. Are mental experiences the causes or effects of physical brain phenomena (where cause and effect are different and consecutive phenomena), or might mental experiences be constituted (or constituents) of physical brain phenomena (therefore co-existing and identical)? Or might the relationship be different?

> *Constituents can be organized (constituted) into different composites (H_2O molecules could exist in the form of water vapor or ice or other states), but a composite can exist only if its constituents exist and are arranged (constituted) in the form of the composite. The constituents don't (consecutively) cause the composite to exist; the constituents become the composite, and the composite comes into existence when its constituents are constituted in that form. The existence of a composite cannot precede the existence of its constituents. The existence of constituents may, but not necessarily, however, precede the existence of the composite; i.e., the constituents might be constituted in the form of the composite from the time of their instantiation. The consecutive cause of the composite is the consecutive cause of the constitution of the constituents, whatever caused the constituents to be constituted in that form. Although the principles of constitution may be understood, the particular constitution of almost any particular physical composite at the human scale is far too complex to be understood with any precision in terms of its elementary physical constituents, but the composite can be understood in terms of principles that have nothing to do with constituents, that are imprecise in comparison with the constituents, and that are subject to numerous anomalies. This imprecise and anomaly-prone understanding of a composite is the approximation referred to above. (The understanding of the simplest physical system in terms of its physical elements may never be free of anomalies because what is considered a physical element at any given time may itself be a composite of more elementary [but unknown] physical constituents, and the understanding of what is considered a physical element may be an approximation of the behavior of the more elementary physical constituents, ad infinitum.)*

To identify a constitutional relationship between a particular constituent and a composite, one must, in principle, be able simultaneously (1) to identify the particular constituent, (2) to identify the particular composite, and (3) either (a) to analyze the composite into constituents of which the particular constituent is one or (b) to synthesize the particular constituent with others into the composite.

The laws of physics identify physical elements and describe the principles by which the properties of those physical elements cause change to one another over time, whether or not the causation is definitive or ambiguous. Every physical phenomenon is an effect with physical causes deriving from the properties of physical elements, but the physical elements and their properties are themselves taken as given (i.e., without cause and incapable of further analysis or explanation) until more elementary physical elements are identified or until the principles are displaced by more general principles, *ad infinitum*. This is the objective-scientific perspective. From the elemental perspective, one adopts the laws of physics as a basis for choosing behavior in specific circumstances where they are efficacious. The physical elements and their properties, however, are not taken as given and incapable of further analysis or explanation. Rather, they too are subject to analysis and explanation in terms of mental experiences, i.e., in terms of external sensory experiences and concepts derived from external sensory experiences. From the elemental perspective, whatever one might identify as physical elements are also composites, the constituents of which are mental elements, i.e., external sensory experiences and concepts making sense of external sensory experiences. Unlike physical constituents, no constituents more elementary than elemental mental experiences will be identified.

UNDERSTANDING

The term "understanding" suggests that there is something that is understood. Since one experiences nothing else, the only things that can be understood are experiences (or composites of experiences). Understanding then takes place by means of concepts that are also experiences.

Concepts are logical relations that one creates between experiences. An experience is understood to the extent that it is conceptually related to other experiences. There are degrees of understanding. Understanding is not an absolute. The minimum level of understanding of an experience (E1) is that it be logically related to a second experience (E2) by a concept (C[E1-E2]) which is a separate intellectual experience whose content embodies the logical relationship drawn by the intellect between E1 and E2. In the notation C[E1-E2], the hyphen symbolizes a particular logic, and other symbols (=, +, >) represent different logics. There is greater understanding of E1 if, in addition to being conceptually related to E2 by C[E1-E2], it is also conceptually related to a third experience (E3) by another concept (C[E1+E3]). There would be yet greater understanding of E1 if C[E1-E2] were itself part of a concept created from itself and C[E1+E3] which would be styled C{C[E1-E2]>C[E1+E3]}. The larger the network of interrelated concepts within which an experience is a member, the more that experience is said to be understood. It is the conceptual network that constitutes the understanding of the experiences of which the network is composed.

Philosophy is the effort to articulate the organizing principles of ever larger, logically coherent conceptual networks — in other words, to achieve profundity. (See Efficacy, Chapter Three.) To achieve profundity may be the object of philosophy, but from one's elemental perspective, profundity is not an end in itself. Rather, one engages in philosophical contemplation to serve one's larger purpose: to maximize value. One adopts a concept to choose behavior only when one conceives that the adoption of that concept will be efficacious: that its adoption now will achieve more value in the future than any other concept. Profundity is only one of three criteria on which efficacy is based. The other two are facility and elegance. Philosophical contemplation is the only circumstance where profundity always trumps facility and elegance. In other circumstances, facility or elegance may be more efficacious. Thus, in practical circumstances, the concepts of practical reality are conceived to be efficacious despite numerous logical inconsistencies and discontinuities (see Natural Concepts of Practical Reality, Chapter Three).

The circumstances in which one conceives that the adoption of a concept will maximize value are its domain, and every concept, no matter how bizarre or absurd, has some domain. Consider the concept "I am the pharaoh of Egypt." Each of the words of that composite concept can be understood separately as representing concepts that are consistent with one's concept of practical reality, but the composite concept "I am the pharaoh of Egypt" contradicts one's practical self-concept and is a practical absurdity. Even that absurdity, however, has a domain of efficacy as, for example, in a private day dream, when writing fiction, when trying to understand ancient history. Even absurdities have important domains. For example, to recognize that an absurd concept contradicts a practical concept is itself an important adoption of them both. When one fantasizes oneself in the position of another person, one vicariously attributes to that person the emotions that one experiences. That vicarious fantasy (a practical absurdity) is the basis on which one presumes to understand the subjective experiences of others — a large and important domain that is a foundation of social relations. What I call "circumstances" are themselves concepts, and therefore domains are concepts. The identification of every concept with its own domain is, at base, an internal organization of all concepts.

For the philosophy of elementalism, no concept has the property of being philosophically "true" or "valid" in the sense of "corresponding with actual reality" or "having universal applicability." Rather, every concept has a domain of efficacy, and what is important is to properly define the domain. A contradiction between two concepts does not imply that one of them must be discarded; rather, within their proper domains, each can be efficaciously adopted. When comparing two apparently contradictory concepts, the problem is not to identify which, if either, is true or false; rather, the problem is to define their respective domains and to determine if the present circumstance is in one of those domains. For elementalism, it is entirely understandable that the concept that one adopts in one practical circumstance might, in some respect, contradict the concept that one adopts in a different circumstance because each may be the most efficacious for the respective circumstance. The full understanding of contradictory concepts requires not merely the definition of the domain of each but also an explanation of the mutual exclusivity of the domains. Only if the present circumstance happens to involve philosophical contemplation of the structure of knowledge is the goal to achieve value by describing the grandest conceptual structure with the fewest contradictions. For elementalism, this philosophical goal is not achieved by identifying true or valid concepts and discarding the remainder. Rather, it is achieved by recognizing that all elemental experiences are organized in the form of mentation such that the experience of every concept logically solves a problem posed by that organization. Though every concept is logical in the overall mentational context, any two concepts may be inconsistent in another respect. That inconsistency (when the inconsistency is itself experienced as a concept), however, is also the solution to a problem posed by mentation; furthermore, the concept that recognizes the inconsistency itself reflects an efficacious adoption of the inconsistent concepts.

Perhaps the most famous example of two contradictory concepts that are efficaciously adopted in adjoining but mutually exclusive domains involves the wave/particle properties of quanta. Physicists would like to conceive a coherent model to predict the behavior of elementary physical particles at the quantum scale, but in the absence of a model without contradictions, physicists adopt a bifurcated model which includes the fewest contradictions. That is, they have defined with some clarity the circumstances in which the wave side of the model is efficacious and other circumstances in which to adopt the particle side.

Question: If philosophy is the effort to create the largest conceptual network with the fewest contradictions, how does the philosophy of elementalism resolve the contradiction between "1 + 1 = 2" and "1 + 1 = 3" without discarding the latter?

Answer: There are circumstances in which every concept is efficacious. Where the "natural number system" is efficacious: 1 + 1 = 2; 1 + 1 does not equal 3; and 1 + 1 = 2 contradicts 1 + 1 = 3. Even in those "natural number" circumstances, recognizing that 1 + 1 = 3 contradicts 1 + 1 = 2 is an important adoption of 1 + 1 = 3. The contradiction between those two sums is not resolved by incorporating 1 + 1 = 3 into the natural number system with status equal to that of 1 + 1 = 2. Rather, elementalism recognizes the possibility of other circumstances in which the natural number system does not apply, in which 1 + 1 = 3 might have an equal or even larger domain than 1 + 1 = 2. Furthermore, elementalism recognizes that there are other contexts, unrelated to the natural number system, where the statements of those two sums do not contradict. The concept 1 + 1 = 3 is properly excluded from the confines of the coherent conceptual network called the "natural number system" in the domain where that system is efficacious, but that network is a small part of the totality of all potentially efficacious conceptual networks. All concepts are logical in relation to the problem each was created to solve, and all are organized to serve the function of maximizing value within the context of mentation. Within the organization of all experiences, all concepts are equal in their full logicality and potential efficacy.

No doubt there is an important practical domain in which it is efficacious to adopt the concept that mental experiences are physically constituted (for example, neurosurgery). The mind/matter problem is not only to define that domain but more important, philosophically, to compare the profundity of the concept of physical constitution of mental experience with the profundity of the elemental model. (See Domains Compared, Chapter Seven.)

Scientific Standard of Understanding

Scientists consider a physical phenomenon to be understood if its occurrences can be described as being effects caused by, and constituted of, particular physical elements identified with some degree of precision and behaving according to the laws of physics, but only to the extent that that description provides diverse predictions with a satisfying degree of reliability, only to the extent of its domain of efficacy. This is the standard of scientific understanding. The more elementary the physical elements in terms of which a phenomenon can be analyzed (the more levels of elementariness in the understanding), the "deeper" the understanding is said to be. The more phenomena at the same level of elementariness are involved in an understanding, the "broader" it is said to be.

Currently, different examples of physical phenomena can be analyzed into physical elements with greater or lesser degrees of refinement and precision, and to that extent the different examples are understood to a greater or lesser degree according to the scientific standard. Since the beginning of science, scientists have sought to identify yet more elementary elements but can conceive no way to identify ultimately elementary physical elements. Each time more elementary physical elements are identified, those new elements are incorporated into the model of external reality, the conceptual network expands, and the scientific standard of understanding deepens accordingly. Much of the recent history of science concerns physical elements being supplanted by more elementary elements that are introduced by technologically increased powers of observation.

Elemental Standard of Understanding
The understanding of a phenomenon satisfies the elemental standard if that understanding provides a consistent analysis of the phenomenon into constituent elemental mental experiences that one is incapable of supplanting with more elementary constituents. An elemental understanding of physical phenomena includes, and does not contradict, the scientific standard of understanding. The elemental understanding of a physical phenomenon includes the elemental understanding of the physical elements in addition to the entire scientific understanding. This additional level of analysis is the extent to which an elemental understanding is deeper and more profound than a scientific one.

Pragmatic Standard of Understanding
To a non-scientist trying to cope with the practicalities of life (a coper), a pragmatic understanding has to do with purpose. An example of a coper is a pianist who understands the relationship between piano keys and piano sound to the extent that he is able to satisfy his purpose to use the piano to create music even if he knows nothing about the mechanical, physical, causal relationship between the piano and the music. The pianist's degree of understanding (pragmatic understanding) is efficacious to the extent that it satisfies the pianist's purpose of making music despite the absence of any explanation deeper than the bald assertion by the pianist that depressing the piano keys causes the piano sound. The assertion is bald and the pianist's understanding has minimal

depth or degree, because the cause and the effect are not part of a larger causal network relating other types of experiences. What is asserted is an initial elementary causal relationship that derives from the pianist's direct experiences of both the cause and the effect where the occurrences of the cause followed patterns determined by the pianist's indeterminate volition. One should not minimize the intellectual achievement involved in the pianist's understanding, which relates all the numerous occurrences of piano sounds and piano keys within the pianist's history. Even to conceptualize a piano sound and piano keys requires an immensely complex underlying intellectual edifice. The pianist's understanding seems bald, however, only in comparison with the scientist's understanding, which involves much greater depth. The pianist's pragmatic understanding would not satisfy the criteria of either scientific understanding or elemental understanding.

A pragmatic understanding need not involve causation. For example, the concept of the regularity of the apparent motion of the sun provides a pragmatic basis for prediction in the complete absence of causal explanation.

The pianist conceives the causal relation between keys and sounds with the intention to make music. To make music is not his real purpose, however. Making music is only the present means by which he hopes to achieve his larger purpose of maximizing value.

Is the pianist's pragmatic understanding fundamentally less worthy than the scientist's? The pianist's understanding says nothing about the means by which the depression of the keys causes the sound. His understanding is an initial, elementary causal relationship. Compare this with the scientist's explanation, which would involve a force causing the acceleration of the key, including the molecular structure of the finger on the key and of the key itself and of the forces operating between the molecules. The molecules could be further analyzed into atoms held in the molecular structure by their particular forces, and so forth, down to the subatomic level. The analysis to the subatomic level would cover the whole mechanical arrangement connecting the key to the hammer and the strings and the air surrounding the strings in which the sound travels. All of these physical elements would behave according to forces acting on elementary matter and causing their behavior in time and space, which in the aggregate are recognized as depressed keys and sounds. Until the analysis reaches the quantum level, the relationships between the physical constituents will be described as definitively causal. At the quantum level, the descriptions of the individual constituents will be probabilistic, but the aggregate of the individual quantum events will be statistically recognizable as deterministic at the human scale. Despite the characterization of the relationships as causal, the scientist ultimately will not be able to identify means by which every cause causes every effect. Of course, the scientist's understanding is purely theoretical: he has reason to think that some general principles describe the relations between mole-cules, and so on, but the molecular structure of any particular finger is far too complex for any scientist to understand, and the atomic or subatomic structures in any particular finger are yet more complex. Even if the scien-tist could surmount the complexity of the multiple levels (depth) of physical elementariness, the understandings of the scientist and the pianist would still be similar in that they both ultimately equally recognize causation, in the absence of any means by which the causation is achieved. Depth of causal levels of understanding does not circumvent the inherent charac-teristic of causation: one cannot understand the means by which causation is achieved, and for every chain of causation, the elementary causal link is itself without a cause. The worth of an understanding lies not in its depth or breadth but in its efficacy to achieve value. The pianist's means to max-imize value is to make music. For that means, the pianist's understanding is better than the scientist's, because, to make music, the most abbreviated concept best allows the pianist to concentrate on making music.

The scientist hopes to maximize value for himself by identifying the most general principles that explain physical phenomena. Both understandings are equally worthy in regard to the means for which they are adopted to achieve value. For the philosopher, the means to achieve value is to identify the most general principles that explain everything. For that purpose, only the elemental standard can satisfy him because the elemental standard includes both the scientific and the pragmatic standards.

One's concept of practical reality (the concepts that one adopts for most of one's decisions) consists largely of pragmatic understandings whose domains of efficacy are very discretely defined. Only a small part of practical reality consists of scientific understandings, and the domain of efficacy for science is limited to scientific experimentation, the design of sophisticated things like cars, and so on. In comparison with much more facile, pragmatic concepts, a scientific understanding is not efficacious for adoption when athletic agility is required as, for example, driving a car or playing a piano. Even though scientific understanding has a limited domain of efficacy, that small domain potentially includes a theoretical understanding of all physical phenomena. It is a domain that is small but embodies great profundity. The domain of efficacy of elemental understandings of physical phenomena is even smaller than that of scientific understandings. It is valuable only for philosophical contemplation, and that domain, which includes all of science, is smaller but includes greater profundity than the domain of science. But elementalism includes more than science. The largest part of the domain of elementalism is the analysis of psychological phenomena, which is a very large domain.

EXPLANATION

An explanation of a phenomenon is the description of constituent or causal relations of which the phenomenon is the composite or effect. Thus the scientific standard of understanding is satisfied if the phenomenon has an explanation deriving from elementary physical properties that provides diverse, reliable predictions. The elemental standard of understanding is satisfied if all the occurrences of the phenomenon have a consistent explanation deriving from elemental mental properties. However, a pragmatic understanding may involve no explanation whatever but merely a historical pattern that provides a satisfying level of prediction as, for example the behavior of the sun.

CHAPTER SIX

DO PHYSICAL PHENOMENA CONSTITUTE OR CAUSE MENTAL EXPERIENCE?

DO PHYSICAL PHENOMENA CONSTITUTE MENTAL EXPERIENCE?

T HE fundamental thesis of this book, elementalism, is that elemental mental experiences are the ultimate elements from which everything else is constituted and into which anything else can be analyzed.

Whether or not there is an actual physical world that corresponds to one's concept of it, one must recognize that what one identifies as a physical phenomenon is constituted from particular types of mental elements, from external sensory experiences and concepts that logically relate external sensory experiences.

One's understanding of the constitutional structure of composites is hierarchical. Elements can be synthesized into composites, and composites can by analyzed into elements. Elements, however, cannot be analyzed into composites, nor can composites be synthesized into elements. One's elemental experiences are the foundation-level constituent elements from which all composites are composed, including the composites that one identifies as physical elements. Since elements cannot be analyzed into composites, mental experiences cannot be analyzed

ELEMENTALISM AND THE MIND/MATTER PROBLEM

into physical elements. One cannot, therefore, explain one's mental elements as being constituted of what one identifies as physical elements. This speaks only to the relationships that one's intellect is capable of drawing with logical consistency. The hierarchical logic by which one understands elements to be constituted into composites prevents an analysis of mental experiences (which are elements) into physical phenomena (which are composites constituted from mental elements). There might be other constitutional logics that are not hierarchical, but I have no experience of such a logic. If, as it seems to me, the analysis of composites must obey the logic of hierarchies, then physical brain phenomena cannot be understood to be constituents of mental experiences in the way that physical elements are the constituents of composite physical phenomena. Water may be identical with (constituted from) a bunch of H_2O molecules, but one has no logic by which to understand how mental experiences might be identical with the activity of a bunch of brain cells. Rather, what one identifies as "brain cells" can only be understood as identical with constituent mental experiences.

One's logic prevents conclusions about an "actual" physical world that might exist independent of one's mental experiences. There may be such an "actual" physical world that corresponds to one's conceptual model of it in some way that one cannot verify. In that world, there may be "actual" physical elements into which mental experiences might be analyzable if only there were someone to do the analysis who, unlike oneself, was not confined to his own experiences, not confined to his own elemental perspective, and not subject to logical limitations similar to one's own. One could not understand that chain of analysis because what one identifies as physical phenomena are constituted from one's mental elements, and the hierarchical logic of constitutions permits only composites to be analyzed into constituents, but not vice versa. One's inescapable elemental perspective and the inherent logic of one's intellect prevent one from analyzing mental experience into more elementary constituents, particularly into physical constituents, which are composites constituted from one's mental elements.

One may experience concepts of physical elements that are the constituents of all physical phenomena (including the brain which one can conceive as the locus of mental experiences), but those physical elements are not elemental in relation to the elements of mentality. On the contrary, the elements of physics are composites constituted from one's elemental mental experiences. Within the confines of one's understanding of physical phenomena, physical elements may be elementary, but those confines do not include mental experiences. The physical sciences continue to be silent concerning mental experiences. Within the larger, unconfined elemental reality, what one considers to be physical elements are not elementary. Rather, they are very compositive composites. The larger, unconfined elemental reality includes what one calls "physical phenomena."

From the practical scientific perspective, there is a hierarchical order of compositivity of organizations of physical matter: (1) at the quantum scale, the elementary forms of matter constituting one's brain are very small compared with (2) the human scale in which human bodies and brains exist but in which the elementary forms of matter are contained. That human scale is itself very small compared with (3) the cosmic scale, which contains the human and the quantum scales. However, from one's elemental perspective, the elementary forms of matter, the structure of brains, and the great cosmic forms are all elaborate conceptual structures that are more or less equidistant in compositivity from the initiating experiences that are the foundation-level elements of which these elaborate structures are composed.

One is left with a conceptual model of the physical world in which the correspondence between particular physical phenomena within one's brain and one's mental experiences may suggest a constitutive relationship, but one is intellectually prevented from conceiving how the physical phenomena (or anything else) might be constituents of mental experiences. This is a limitation that derives from one's inescapable elemental perspective and is not a defect or a paradox. Furthermore, as the next section demonstrates, it is a limitation that may have no practical significance apart from its place in philosophical reflection.

The innumerable individual sensory experiences that one experiences over a lifetime and individual concepts that make sense of them are the elemental basis on which stands the conceptual structure called "one's model of physical reality," of which the laws of physics are the peak. For reasons of efficacy, those individual experiences are either forgotten or relegated to deep background details, but they remain the hidden elemental substructural foundation of which one's model of physical reality is a superstructure. Within the superstructure, and provided that one disregards the substructure, the elements of physics are elementary and the laws of physics may be exhaustive. For reasons of efficacy, one properly learns to disregard the substructure in practical circumstances. Unless one is considering philosophical mind/matter issues, one does well to forget about the elemental substructure of one's concepts of practical physical reality because awareness of the substructure would impair the speed of one's decision-making. The laws of physics cannot provide an explanation of any part of the substructure on which the laws stand, much less of the elements of the substructure.

A different approach leads to the same conclusion. To say that mental experiences in general are constituted from brain phenomena is to say that each mental experience is constituted from particular brain phenomena. To identify a constitutional relationship between a particular composite and a constituent, one must, in principle, be able simultaneously (1) to identify the particular composite, (2) to identify the particular constituent, and (3) either (a) to analyze the composite into constituents of which the particular constituent is one or (b) to synthesize the particular constituent with others into the composite.

To identify the constitutional relation between a particular physical phenomenon and particular mental experiences, one must, in principle, be able to identify the particular physical phenomenon.

Whatever one might identify as a particular physical phenomenon (PPP), the identification occurs by means of particular external sensory experiences (PESE) and particular concepts (PC) that interpret those sensory experiences to be the physical phenomenon. There is nothing more to PPP than

PESE and PC by which PPP is identified. PPP has no properties other than the attributes of PESP and PC that constitute its identification. What holds for any particular physical phenomenon holds for all. The identification of a physical phenomenon at once identifies its constituent experiences and includes both the analysis of the physical phenomenon into constituent experiences and the synthesis of the constituents into the composite that one identifies as the physical phenomenon. This demonstrates that any particular physical phenomenon, PPP, is constituted from particular experiences PESE and PC, but it does not demonstrate that PPP is not a constituent of other experiences. For PPP to be a constituent of other experiences, PESE and PC would be constituents of those other experiences. Those other experiences, therefore, would be composites. Elemental experiences, however, are not composed of other experiences or of anything else. (The elemental character of elemental experiences cannot be proven, it can only be recognized and serve as the basis for proof of other concepts.) Ergo, physical phenomena are not the constituents of mental experiences.

DO PHYSICAL PHENOMENA CAUSE MENTAL EXPERIENCE?

Though conceptual limitations must be rigidly respected for philosophical purposes, might there be a practical way efficaciously to disregard or circumvent the limitations? What practical understanding might be achieved by disregarding the hierarchical constitutional limitation and nevertheless trying to identify physical constituents of mental experiences?

The conceptual limitations imposed by the hierarchical nature of constitutionality do not apply to probable consecutive causation. Probable consecutive causation implies nothing about the nature of the cause or of the effect and suggests only that instantiating the cause in the future will probably be followed by the effect. What understanding of the (probable consecutive) causal relations between physical brain phenomena and mental experiences might be achieved?

Might such understandings "solve the mystery of the organization of mental experiences" by providing a scientifically precise model of mentality?

Consider the following thought experiment.

Imagine:

1. A scientist with state-of-the-art understanding of brain physics and neuro-surgery wants to investigate the relationship between physical activity in the brain and mental experience.

2. The scientist cannot investigate brains in general; he must start somewhere in particular. Imagine, therefore, that he starts with one particular brain that belongs to a particular person called "the subject."

3. The scientist applies the techniques of physics to investigate the physical nature of the subject's brain and, to the degree of refinement that the state of the art allows, the scientist identifies physical elements in the subject's brain that relate to one another according to the laws of physics in the same way that similar physical elements do in any other circumstance. The scientist makes a list of all the physical phenomena that he observes. Every item in this list is a description of a physical phenomenon, and that description is similar to the physical descriptions of anything else that physicists describe with diagrams and symbols and mathematical equations. Like the equations and diagrams that physicists use to describe their usual subject matter, from lasers to quarks to pulsars, nothing in the equations or diagrams that describe the physical phenomena observed in the subject's brain has any mental attributes. The items on the list are purely physical phenomena. At the individual quantum scale, the phenomena are different each time they are observed. Imagine, however, at the scale of anatomical brain structures, that the physical phenomena exhibit causally exhaustive determinacy, and it is these human-scale phenomena that the scientist enters on his list. Each item on the list is completely self-contained, in the sense that the description of any physical phenomenon includes all its causes and all its effects, all of which are physical, just the same as the description of any other physical phenomena.

4. The scientist wants to determine if any of the entries on the list relates to a mental experience. How can he do this? Well, when the scientist observes a particular physical brain phenomenon, he can ask the subject whether the subject is experiencing anything. Whatever the subject answers, the scientist would want to determine (1) whether the subject is intentionally truthful or not; (2) whether, supposing that the subject is intentionally truthful, the subject has words to identify his mental experiences unambiguously or whether the subject's statements should not be relied on because of the subject's limited ability to articulate; and (3) what meaning, assuming that the subject is truthful and articulate, the scientist should give to the subject's statements about the subject's mental experiences. The scientist experiences only his own experiences, not the subject's. Consequently, the scientist cannot conceive any clever way to design the experiment to determine if the words used by subject to describe the subject's experiences have the same meaning to the scientist that they do to the subject. The scientist wants to be strictly objective, and he cannot conceive an experimental design to rule out the possibility that the subject is just an anatomically correct robot that experiences no experiences, instead of a normal person with normal experiences.

5. The scientist decides that he will be both experimenter and subject. Imagine (1) that technology has reached the stage that non-invasive techniques are available to observe the most refined, minute physical events in the brain and (2) that somehow the scientist has overcome the insurmountable problem that "thinking about thinking changes thinking." With himself as the subject, the scientist compiles a long list of physical phenomena that he observes in his own brain, and, once again, each item on the list includes a complete description of all the physical causes and effects and nothing in the physical descriptions suggests anything of a mental nature. The physical events are just statistically significant human-scale aggregates of quarks and anti-neutrinos, and so on, relating to one another according to the laws of physics, exactly as they do on the moon or any place else where causally exhaustive determinacy at

the human-scale applies. The list of physical phenomena is as extensive as the state of the art allows.

6. The scientist is truthful and articulate and this thought experiment is the simplest idealization. Accordingly, for each item on the list of physical phenomena that the scientist observes in his brain, the scientist identifies a particular corresponding mental experience. The correspondence is purely temporal, but there are three basic types of temporal correspondence: physical phenomena preceding mental experience; physical phenomena simultaneous with mental experience; physical phenomena succeeding mental experience. Only the physical-precedes-mental correspondences are candidates for consecutive causation of mental experiences by physical phenomena. The simultaneous correspondences potentially reflect constitutional causation. The physical-succeeding-mental correspondences are candidates for mental causation of physical phenomena or perhaps candidates for a weird quantum explanation. For this simplest ideal thought experiment, assume that the correspondences are all simultaneous with no concerns for relativity — at the time that he observes a particular physical phenomena, the scientist makes note of the simultaneous mental experiences. Of course, the experiences that he experiences when he observes the physical phenomena and makes note of the simultaneous mental experiences will be, *inter alia*, the experiences that constitute the observation and the note-making. These he experiences in his role as experimenter ("experimenter-role experiences"). Any other simultaneous experiences will be those related to his role as subject ("subject-role experiences"). Imagine, in the interest of simplicity, that the scientist is cleverly able to isolate the subject-role experiences and the corresponding physical phenomena, and it is these subject-role experiences and corresponding physical phenomena that he enters on his list. The scientist now has two lists: one list of physical brain phenomena and another list of simultaneous subject-role experiences. Imagine, for simplicity, that each item in either list corresponds to a particular item in the other. Call these two corresponding lists the Table of Correspondences.

7. The scientist organizes the order of items on the list of physical phenomena according to patterns and similarities that he thinks he recognizes in the physical descriptions. He discovers that when the physical list is so organized, the resultant organization of the corresponding mental experiences also seems to embody some organization. For example, in the organized physical list there is a group of phenomena that differ only in the concentrations of a particular chemical at a particular brain location which the scientist has arranged in increasing order of concentration, and the items in the corresponding mental list are described as, for example, experiences of anger of increasing intensity. Another group of physical items that is organized according to, for instance, electrical current passing through adjacent cells turns out to correspond to the concepts of 1, 2, 3 . . . At the conclusion of this organization, the scientist realizes that for every mental experience for which he has a name, he can identify a corresponding physical phenomenon, and that for every physical phenomenon that he observes, he can identify a corresponding mental experience. Furthermore, all the physical phenomena seem to fit into natural groupings that result in what seem to be natural groupings of corresponding mental experiences.

8. The scientist performs the experiment on numerous subjects, and, with a high level of consistency, (1) the scientist observes in their brains the same physical phenomena that he observed in his own brain and that he entered on the physical list, and (2) the subjects report mental experiences in words that correspond to the descriptions of his own mental experiences in the Table of Correspondences. The scientist feels confident that the Table of Correspondences has some general application.

9. The state of the art is such that the scientist can non-injuriously manipulate the most minute and complex physical activity in the brain. The scientist instantiates particular physical phenomena from the Table of Correspondences in the brains of various subjects after which they report mental experiences similar to the corresponding entries in the Table of Correspondences. With the same

technique, the scientist seems able to control the behavior of the subjects. This amounts to a history of effect (report of mental experience) following cause (instantiation of physical brain phenomenon) where the occurrence of the cause followed a random pattern determined only by the scientist's own indeterminate volition. Imagine that he assumes the roles of both experimenter and subject and instantiates physical phenomena in his own brain. The experimenter-role experiences additionally include the experiences involved in instantiating the physical phenomena. Suppose, however, that he is somehow able to distinguish even these experimenter-role experiences from the subject-role experiences, and he recognizes that the instantiation of particular physical brain phenomena precedes the mental experiences that correspond to the experiences in the Table of Correspondences. He concludes that the instantiation of the physical brain phenomena probably caused the mental experiences — that he could rely on a prediction that the mental experience would, in the future, follow the instantiation of the physical brain phenomena.

10. All of the above seems to hold for most of the subjects that the scientist investigates; however, the scientist identifies "anomalous" physical phenomena in some subjects who are considered by psychiatrists to be mentally ill. He eliminates the anomalies surgically, and the subjects are no longer considered mentally ill.

What implications can the scientist draw from the Table of Correspondences and about the reliability of the predictions that it facilitates?

(a) The simultaneous occurrences of physical phenomena and mental experiences are consistent with a constitutional relationship, but are utterly ambiguous as to which might be the constituent and which the composite. Nothing about the Table of Correspondences analyzed or synthesized either mental experiences or physical phenomena. Any conclusions about the constitutional relationship

DO PHYSICAL PHENOMENA CONSTITUTE OR CAUSE MENTAL EXPERIENCE?

between them, therefore, would be unwarranted philosophically. Furthermore, it is difficult to imagine what practical efficacy there might derive from assuming the relationship to be constitutional without identifying which is the constituent and which the composite. Practical efficacy usually derives from facility and elegance over profundity, and to call a temporal correspondence between two otherwise unrelated phenomena by the name "constitutional relationship" in which the constituent and the composite are not identified seems to introduce confusion and complexity, not facility or elegance.

(b) Does the Table of Correspondences constitute an understanding of the relationship between mental experiences and physical brain phenomena? The physical descriptions included all physical causes and effects, and the mental experiences were not among them. The Table of Correspondences does not establish that mental experiences are constituted of physical phenomena, and therefore does not qualify as a scientific understanding of the relationship between them. However, if the Table provided reliable predictions sufficient to afford a basis for the scientist to "induce" experiences, control behavior, and surgically cure mental illness with a high degree of predictive reliability, the Table of Correspondences would qualify as a pragmatic understanding for those purposes. Experimentally determining that the consecutivity of the instantiation of a physical brain phenomenon followed by a mental experience persists even when the occurrence of that physical phenomenon is indeterminate (because it was induced by the indeterminate volition of the scientist) makes logical the conclusion that the instantiation of the physical phenomenon is the probable cause of the experience.

Could the scientist declare that the mental experiences emerged from the corresponding physical phenomena in the Table of Correspondences so as to be newly observed physical properties of the elementary physical constituents of those phenomena? The Table of Correspondences listed physical phenomena that the scientist observed in his own brain that corresponded with mental experiences that the scientist experienced (ignoring the problem that "thinking about thinking changes thinking"). The scientist was unable to draw correspondences between his observations of the brains of other subjects and the mental experiences of those subjects because he could not observe the experiences of the other subjects. One experiences only one's own experiences, and the scientist had no evidence that the other people experienced experiences at all. He could only hypothesize that those subjects experienced experiences similar to his own when they reported, in words that he recognized, that they were experiencing experiences similar to those that appeared in the Table of Correspondences that related his own experiences to his own brain phenomena. The scientist remained profoundly ignorant of whether the other subjects experienced mental experiences at all. The most that the scientist could conclude logically is that the behavior of the physical entities that he recognized as other persons could be vaguely understood (predicted with modest reliability) as though they experienced their own private mentation, similar to his own. Consequently, the scientist should not declare mental experiences to be physical properties emerging from brains, because his observations of brains other than his own does not disclose any experiences occurring there.

(c) Because each entry on the list of physical phenomena in the Table of Correspondences includes all of the causes and effects of that physical phenomenon, and because those causes and effects are also physical phenomena, all of which are completely describable in terms of physical elements having no mental attributes, the physical events themselves imply nothing about mental experiences. Nothing in the physical description of any particular physical phenomenon leads logically to the corresponding mental experiences, or vice versa. Everything in the list of mental experiences came from the scientist's own introspection in his role as subject independent of the observations of the physical phenomena simultaneously observed by the scientist in his role as experimenter. The only reason that he entered a mental experience on the list adjacent to a particular physical phenomenon was that the mental experience occurred simultaneously with the physical phenomenon and followed the instantiation of the physical phenomenon. With another subject, the entries in the list of mental experiences came from that subject's introspection, independent of the observations by the scientist of the subject's brain physics. The subject came to the experiment with a prior capability of describing his mental experiences, and he could have described his mental experiences whether or not the scientist was observing the physical activity in his brain. The descriptions of the mental experiences could have been elicited whether or not the experiment took place. The capability to describe mental experiences reflected a prior understanding of their identity. If the subject's understanding of the identity of his mental experiences was "incorrect" prior to the experiment, the resulting Table of Correspondences would be incorrect accordingly. There was nothing in the experiment that could distinguish correctly described mental experiences from those that might be incorrectly described. The power, the generality, of probable consecutive causation is that it is applicable in the absence of any understanding of the nature of the particular cause or effect (C or E), but its limitation is that it requires C and E to be defined before the inference of probable causation can be drawn. Furthermore, once it is drawn, the inference reveals nothing about the nature of C or E. Advancement of the state of science and technology can affect only the refinement of the list of physical phenomena in the Table of Correspondences. It cannot affect the articulation of the mental experiences that derives from a prior understanding by the subject of his mental experiences, and that understanding is independent of the state of science. What the experiment achieved was the Table of Correspondences and a basis of future prediction. Even though the Table of Correspondences could form the basis of a valuable pragmatic understanding of the temporal relationship between brain physics and mental experiences for medical or other pragmatic purposes, advances in the understanding of the identity and essential nature of mental experiences will continue to come from introspection, quite apart from the state of physical science. The mystery of the organization of mental experiences will not yield to advances in objective science.

(d) Since an understanding of mental experience is independent of an understanding of brain physics, a table of correspondences that relates physical brain phenomena to corresponding mental experiences is the most complete description that can relate the two. One has no way to relate a physical phenomenon with a mental experience other than by their correspondence in time. The Table of Correspondences consists of two lists of temporally corresponding items that bear no other apparent relationship to each other. A history of temporal correspondence may provide a basis of reliable predictions sufficient for a pragmatic understanding of the relationship between those events, but it can provide no scientific explanation. A history of temporal correspondence of events suggests that one event may be predictable in terms of the other, but not necessarily; i.e., the Table of Correspondences is logically compatible with (1) the idea that physical brain phenomena constitute mental experience in some way that is not understood or (2) the idea that mental experiences animate otherwise sterile physical brain tissue in some way that is not understood or even (3) that the correspondence is purely coincidental.

(e) Depending on the refinement and precision of the items, a table of correspondences, even in the absence of any explanation for the correspondences, can have as much practical value as a full explanation of the correspondences. A scientific explanation of the correspondences between different types of things often provides an elegant means of determining which particular example of one of the types corresponds to any particular example of the other type (for example, a very simple mathematical formula can describe an infinite number of correspondences). If it is complete, therefore, a table of correspondences can provide the same function, but not with the same elegance. Even though a complete table of correspondences would not provide a scientific understanding of the relationship between the corresponding items, that is the only thing that it would not provide.

(f) Science can supply refinement and precision to the items on a list of physical phenomena, but a table of correspondences is only as valuable as the refinement of both sides of the table. Refinement of the descriptions of the mental experiences is independent of the state of science and depends on understanding subjective mental experiences that are accessible only by introspection. Consequently, the value of a table of correspondences depends equally on the sophistication of both of two independent disciplines: brain physics and introspective psychology. Even though the Table of Correspondences provided no insight that the subject did not previously have into the nature of mental experiences, the pragmatic understanding provided by the Table of Correspondences (depending on its degree of completeness) may have as much practical value as a scientific understanding.

(g) In this thought experiment, on the one hand, the scientist observes his own physical brain. Those observations are composed of (1) his own external sensory experiences and (2) his own concepts (intellectual experiences) of what those sensory experiences signify according to his model of external reality. Those observations are themselves mental experiences of the scientist that are experienced by the scientist in his role as experimenter and give rise to the list of physical brain phenomena on one side of the Table of Correspondences. On the other hand, the list of mental experiences that makes up the other side of the Table of Correspondences contains the scientist's mental experiences that he experienced in his role as subject. The scientist cannot escape the conclusion that his own mental experiences are the stuff with which he deals on all sides. The scientist (we are all both scientists and copers) cannot escape his elemental subjective perspective, from which mental experiences are elemental, and what he calls the "physical world" is a logically constituted composite of his own elemental mental experiences.

SUMMARY

(1) Mental experiences have been identified as one's elemental mental experiences and composites thereof described but not defined in the elemental model. (2) What one identifies as physical phenomena are described by the laws of physics, which are part of one's model of external reality, which is a grand intellectual creation (a mental experience) that makes sense of, *inter alia*, one's external sensory experiences. (3) The relationship between mental experiences and physical phenomena is that one's elemental mental experiences are the elemental constituents of what one defines as physical phenomena. Consequently, (4) one cannot explain mental experiences as composites composed of physical elements because (5) one's logic permits analysis only of composites into elements, not vice versa. But (6) these conclusions say nothing about an "actual" world that might exist independent of one's experiences and that corresponds to the laws of physics. In such a world (about which nothing can be known), brain physics may "actually" cause mental experiences. Moreover, (7) these conclusions are not themselves a practical limitation for some purposes because they do not prohibit the development of a history of temporal correspondences between mental experiences and physical brain events that may be efficacious for some purposes, depending on the refinement of the entries on both sides of the table. (8) To the extent that a table of correspondences is developed that provides reliable predictions for medical or neurological purposes, one can profitably proceed, for those purposes, as though physical brain events probably cause mental experiences, even though one is incapable of scientifically understanding that causation. (9) Brain physics itself is necessarily silent as to mental effects, and the advance of science can have no effect on the advance of the understanding of the essential nature of mental experience. Consequently, (10) the refinement and completeness of a useful table of correspondences will depend on independent advancement of both brain physics and introspective psychology.

Philosophically, one must exclude from one's model of external reality the concept that physical brain phenomena (composites) constitute

one's mental experiences (elements), because one's inescapable elemental perspective and one's conceptual limitations prevent one from
understanding such a constitution. Just as there is a blind spot in the
center of one's visual field, one's conceptual limitations give rise to a
blind spot or a gap in one's understanding. The blind spot cannot be
viewed from one's inescapable elemental perspective. One's understanding of the organization of all one's mental experiences (the
universe) is internally consistent only if one recognizes that the organization of external sensory experiences (what one calls "external
reality") is a subdivision within the larger organization, not vice versa.
The understanding is possible only if one recognizes the gap. A blind
spot or a gap in one's understanding is not an inconsistency. Nor does
it represent a practical limitation since it does not preclude the development of a table of correspondences of exquisite refinement. There is,
therefore, potentially great practical benefit in the continuing advance
of brain science, provided that it is matched by advances in introspective psychology, even though such advances will not breach the gap.

CHAPTER SEVEN

DO MENTAL EXPERIENCES CAUSE PHYSICAL PHENOMENA?

I T is hard to imagine a practical principle more important or more general than the concept that each person is responsible for his intended actions. Call that the principle of "individual responsibility." (The responsibility referred to in the principle of individual responsibility is not necessarily moral responsibility, that is, responsibility for the intended consequences of one's actions. Rather, individual responsibility is simply causal responsibility for having taken the action.) The principle of individual responsibility consists of two parts: (1) the principle of "personal responsibility" (first-person responsibility), whereby certain types of behavior of one's body are caused by one's volition, and (2) the principle of "responsibility of others" (second- and third-person responsibility), whereby certain types of behavior of other people are caused by their individual volitions. From the practical perspective, volition is a mental phenomenon, and bodily behavior is a physical phenomenon. The general practical principle of individual responsibility therefore suggests that some mental experiences cause physical effects, and brings into question the exhaustivity of the laws of physics, by which only physical causes have physical effects.

Even from the practical perspective, one experiences only one's own experiences. One can best predict the behavior of the bodies of other people by adopting the concept that they experience experiences similar to those that one imagines one would experience in their circumstances. However, they might be sophisticated robots without experiences, and science may reach the stage that the behavior of other people may be predictable in purely physical terms, as a consequence of physical phenomena within their brain/body systems, without reference to their experiences or volition — as though they were robots. Consequently, only the first part of the principle of individual responsibility (personal responsibility whereby one's own volition causes the behavior of one's body) challenges the exhaustivity of the laws of physics. Other people may not have the experiences that constitute volition, whereas one cannot deny one's own experiences.

This chapter identifies the particular elemental experiences that are included in both parts of the principle of individual responsibility and then considers whether genuine problems remain.

PERSONAL RESPONSIBILITY FOR ONE'S BODILY BEHAVIOR

The principle of personal (first person) responsibility can be divided into three parts: (1) "one's volition," (2) "causes," and (3) "one's bodily behavior."

Volition
"One's volition" is one's intentional effort to behave in a particular way (the effort to do what one wants to do) and is analyzable into the experiences contained in stages 3, 4, and 5 within a unit of mentation. Each unit represents a separate volition. In stage 3, one experiences emotions and the hierarchy of strategic behavioral desires arranged in order of the intensity of each emotion. Within the concept "what one wants to do," the hierarchy of desires is the elemental basis of "one wants." In stage 4, one experiences the decision: the concept that identifies the one behavior that will maximally implement the desires. The decision is the elemental basis of "what to do." This decision includes the identification of the particular learned mental output (the particular direction and intensity of concentration) that will cause the behavior that one has decided to attempt. In stage 5, one experiences concentra-

tion focusing on the appropriate learned output to implement the decision: the intensity of concentration is the effort. Volition (intentional
effort to behave in a particular way) is the composite of three types of
experiences within one unit of mentation: the emotions; the concept
how to behave, including the identification of the learned output that
will cause that behavior; and the concentration on that output. The
three types are experienced sequentially within one unit of mentation.
In stage 1 of the next unit of mentation, one experiences external sensory experiences and internal bodily experiences, which one conceives
to be the behavior of one's body in response to the volition in the previous unit. Of course, the emotions in stage 3 arise only in consequence
of the concept of reality created in stage 2, and that concept is created
only to interpret the feelings experienced in stage 1.

It is important to recognize that volition is restricted to behaviors corresponding to the inventory of learned outputs. For example, if while
learning how to play the violin one caused the instrument to screech,
one would be personally responsible for the general fact of the screech
because one intentionally undertook to play the violin without knowing
how to do it sweetly. One would not, however, be responsible for the
particular screech (for the particular bodily movements that led to the
particular screech) because one did not know how to make one's body
behave correctly and one could not repeat the particular screech. The
particulars of the screech would be considered the random effect of
incompetence rather than the effect of an act of volition. A learned
output is a particular direction and intensity of concentration that one
conceives will probably cause particular bodily behavior. Furthermore,
the conception of the direction, the intensity, and the resultant behavior
have to be clear enough that when one decides to implement that
behavior, concentration automatically focuses correctly often enough
that one is confident that one has learned the behavior. Each learned
behavior, each learned output, reflects a concept of a mental location
and of the reliability of that concept in causing the appropriate
behavior. The circumstances in which one has confidence in one's
ability to behave in a particular way constitute the domain of adoption

of the concept of the learned output that causes that behavior. Volition (hence the principle of personal responsibility) is limited to the domains of the concepts that define one's learned behaviors.

> *Normally, a unit of mentation lasts in the order of one half of a second, the duration of the present. A new volition is formed, at most, a few times per second. Over longer terms, the history of volitions within numerous individual units of mentation reveals coherent longer-term purposes in the same way that classical Newtonian physics emerges as a useful approximation of large aggregates of quantum phenomena. Newtonian-scale purpose is demonstrated in the following examples: (1) the fifteen seconds during which one sprints to avoid the attack of a lion, (2) the few hours during which one demonstrates a coherent purpose on a golf course, and (3) a life-time during which the longest-term strategy, social philosophy, and so on, emerge. The coherent "purpose" demonstrated during these Newtonian terms is an aggregate made up of individual volitions within numerous units of mentation. Furthermore, in the course of executing a Newtonian-scale purpose such as playing golf, one may experience numerous volitional behaviors that are unrelated to that purpose (for example, conversation with one's golf mates), and there will also be much non-volitional behavior such as perspiring or grimacing.*

In what follows, the term "volition," in the singular, refers to the volition experienced within one unit of mentation, and the plural "volitions" refers to the separate volitions experienced within separate units. Similarly, the term "behavior," in the singular, refers to the behavior caused by one mental output unit, and the plural refers to the separate behaviors caused by separate output units.

Causation
The description of causation in general is addressed in Chapter Five, above.

One's Bodily Behavior
One's bodily behavior is a physical phenomenon. Chapter Five, above, addresses physical phenomena in general, but one's bodily behavior is a specific physical phenomenon with specific additional elemental attributes.

The totality of one's external sensory experiences and the concepts making sense of them constitute one's model of all things physical. Any particular physical phenomenon is analyzable into the particular concept of that particular phenomenon and the particular sensory experiences that form the basis for that particular concept. The particular concepts draw on the overall model of physical reality, and vice versa. One's bodily behavior is similarly analyzable into the external sensory experiences that one conceives to represent one's physical body behaving in space and time, but additionally there are internal bodily experiences (such as proprioception and the sensation of muscle contraction) that one also conceives to represent attributes of the behavior of one's body. The elemental experiences into which "the behavior of one's body" can be analyzed are external sensory experiences, internal bodily experiences, and the concepts that coherently interpret both types of feelings as the behavior of one's body.

The three parts of the practical principle (volition, causation, and bodily behavior) have now been individually described in elemental terms. What now is the logic whereby the parts are combined in the form "one's volition causes one's bodily behavior" (the principle of personal responsibility)?

One experiences the elements that make up the parts of the principle sequentially. The emotions in stage 3 precede the decision how to behave in stage 4. The decision precedes the effort to activate an output in stage 5, which precedes the feelings in stage 1 of the next unit of mentation that one interprets in stage 2 as the behavior of one's body. Consider the sequence "effort to behave (concentration on an output) precedes the experiences that one interprets as bodily behavior." This effort/behavior consecutivity is not absolute, but it is reliable enough to provide a basis for prediction. Consecutivity is not sufficient to infer causation unless the effort is indeterminate. Is there any reason to regard the effort as indeterminate?

Effort always succeeds a decision to exert the effort. Is there any reason to consider the decision to be indeterminate? Yes. The decision is a concept of the single behavior that will maximally implement all the behavioral desires. One does not experience the process of conceptualization or reasoning. All concepts emerge complete into consciousness. Only after a concept has been experienced can one recognize the logic according to which the concept solves the problem posed to the intellect, the logic according to which the concept relates the experiences that it relates. One cannot predict what concepts one will experience: the occurrence of any particular conceptual experience is genuinely indeterminate. Like all concepts, the decision how to behave is indeterminate. Furthermore, since the effort to behave (concentration on a particular output) reliably follows the decision, one reasonably infers that the decision probably causes the effort (consecutivity despite indeterminacy).

Intentional effort always follows decisions. One does not find oneself making intentional efforts to behave without having decided to attempt the particular behavior. Effort refers to intensity of concentration, but the direction and intensity of concentration do not always achieve the behavior that one intends. For example, when one tries to learn a new behavior one makes numerous attempts to identify the correct direction and intensity of concentration, but one recognizes the correct direction and intensity only when one experiences the subsequent external sensory and internal bodily experiences that one interprets as the intended behavior of one's body. The whole history of consecutivities involved in learning behaviors is the basis on which one concludes that a decision to attempt a particular behavior causes the following effort and direction of concentration on a particular output, which in turn causes the subsequent behavior of one's body.

It is important to emphasize that there are specific types of behavior that do not seem to be caused by intentional efforts and that not all intentional efforts are followed by the intended behavior. Sneezing, coughing, crying, smiling, and so on are examples of behavior that can occur without volition, and every athlete knows that the same intended effort on one day does not produce the same level of behavior the next. One recognizes the general principle that particular efforts cause particular behaviors, but one also recognizes exceptions to that general principle. One develops an inventory of concepts identifying particular behaviors that, in particular circumstances, succeed concentration on particular mental locations (outputs) and of concepts identifying other behaviors that correspond with something else.

The concept that one's intentional effort probably causes one's bodily behavior may be the very first initial, elementary, probable, consecutively causal relationship that one identifies. If so, that initial elementary causal relationship is the foundation on which one's entire intellectual causal network logically stands. The identification of that initial causal relationship was based on the concept that volition is indeterminate. The idea that volition is an effect of physical brain phenomena (along with causal exhaustivity) implies that volition is determinate. If so, one's initial elementary causal relationship (the foundation of all others) is in jeopardy, and the entire structure of causal relationships that one recognizes may be philosophically undermined, including (for the scientist manipulating a subject's brain) the concept that brain phenomena cause mental experiences. As a practical matter, however, one is not forced to resolve this paradox because one is able to adopt apparently contradictory concepts within separate domains. Only philosophers engaged in philosophical contemplation are obliged to resolve all inconsistencies.

The indeterminate intellectual component of one's volition permits one to conceive the principle of personal responsibility (one's volition causes one's bodily behavior), and the adoption of that principle is efficacious for most practical purposes. It is crucial to remember that the inference of causation as an explanation of consecutive phenomena does not prove unambiguous causation. The inference of causation can never serve to prove unambiguous causation in any particular case. Rather, it serves only as a basis to choose a concept to be adopted for future decisions. In this case, the inference of personal responsibility does not prove that the mental experiences included in one's volition definitively cause the physical behavior of one's body. Rather, the inference of personal responsibility implies only that one conceives that one's concepts identifying the behavioral significance of particular learned outputs (in comparison with one's other concepts) probably will maximize value if adopted within their proper domains.

One adopts the principle of personal responsibility for most practical purposes because of its efficacy, but this general principle is the result of two efficacious simplifications: (1) causation has been simplified to exclude the probable aspect, and (2) volition, at the Newtonian scale, has been simplified into a unitary entity instead of an aggregate of specific volitions. The practical, simplified version is efficacious for most practical Newtonian-scale circumstances (the domain of the simplified version), but it is inefficacious for fundamental philosophical analysis (in which efficacy derives only from profundity) because personal responsibility contradicts the possible determinacy of the behavior of one's body implied by causal exhaustivity, which determinacy also has a domain. The contradiction is resolved by recognizing (1) the hypothetical ambiguous character of causation and (2) that the domain of personal responsibility is separate from the domain within which the concept of determinate bodily behavior is efficacious. (See Domains Compared, below.)

RESPONSIBILITY OF OTHERS FOR THE BEHAVIOR OF THEIR BODIES

In most practical circumstances, one also adopts the simplified concept that the volitional behavior of other people is caused by their individual volitions, but, in comparison with the principle of personal responsibility, the responsibility of others for their volitional behavior has an additional elemental substructure. The concept that other people have experiences at all is derived from a fantasy. A fantasy is a sequence of concepts (for example, a dream) in which one identifies oneself as a participant but in which the concepts do not cohere with the larger structure of concepts that one calls memories. One fantasizes oneself in the circumstances of another person, and those fantastic concepts give rise to emotional experiences of one's own. The fact that one knows that the fantasy is a fantasy can be said to distort the resultant emotions in the sense that they would be different if one conceived that one were actually (not just vicariously) in the circumstances of the other person. For example, the emotions caused by the fantasy may be less intense than those one would experience if one conceived the fantasy were real. One fantasizes oneself in the circumstances of another person, and then one conceptually attributes to that other person emotions similar to those that one experiences in consequence of the fantasy. This vicarious, fantastic attribution of one's own emotions to another person leads to the concept that the person will also experience the behavioral desires included in the emotions and will decide, and hence behave, accordingly.

The general principle of individual responsibility (first, second, and third person responsibility for the intended behavior of each individual) is based on (1) the concept that one's volition causes one's bodily behavior and (2) the fantastic attribution to other persons of experiences similar to one's own. For most practical circumstances, the most simplified version of that principle is most efficacious. All reference to the causation being probable, or to the attribution of one's own experiences to another person being fantastic, are efficaciously relegated to deep background, and what remains is the general principle of individual responsibility — that volition (mental experiences) causes bodily behavior (physical phenomena). In yet deeper background are the concepts that what one calls physical reality, including other people, are themselves aggregates of one's elemental experiences.

DOMAINS COMPARED

The thought experiment in Chapter Six postulated that science reaches the stage where a scientist can control the brain activity of his subject and receive reports from the subject that suggest to the scientist that the instantiation of particular brain activity probably causes the subject's mental experiences — assuming that the scientist believes the subject's reports of his experiences. When the scientist manipulates the subject's brain with the intention of causing the subject to experience particular mental experiences, the scientist is testing the concept that the subject's physical brain phenomena probably cause his mental experiences. The scientist does this by instantiating particular physical brain phenomena in a random pattern determined only by the scientist's indeterminate volition and by interpreting the reports from the subject concerning the subject's experiences following each instantiation. If the results of the test demonstrate a history of consecutivity despite indeterminacy, the scientist may adopt the concept that instantiating the physical phenomena in the brain of the subject probably causes the subject's experiences. To the extent that he becomes confident, the scientist may abandon the "probably" part of the concept, and it may become a belief. Call it the "scientist's belief," and it includes the concept that the subject has his own private experiences and the concept that those experiences are caused by instantiating the corresponding physical phenomena within the subject's brain. The domain of adoption of that belief would be confined to circumstances comparable to the history, i.e., confined to circumstances comparable to the experiment.

At the same time that the scientist adopts his belief about the cause of the subject's experiences, however, he is manipulating the physical brain phenomena of the subject by means of some behavior of his (the scientist's) own body. That is, the scientist is manipulating some surgical apparatus by means of his own bodily behavior. For the purpose of manipulating the apparatus, the scientist is adopting the concept of his own personal responsibility: that his own indeterminate volition causes his own bodily behavior. The domain of that concept (the scientist's personal responsibility, which is surely a belief) is any circumstance in which the scientist wants and expects his body to behave. Call the belief in personal responsibility one's "personal belief." The scientist is at once a scientist and an ordinary person, and he can adopt both a personal belief and a scientist's belief at the same time.

One way to define the mind/matter problem is in terms of the apparent contradiction between the personal belief and the scientist's belief: the personal belief considers that some mental experiences cause physical phenomena; the scientist's belief considers that some physical phenomena cause mental experiences. Do these beliefs represent a genuine contradiction, and if so, what is its significance?

Both the personal and the scientist's beliefs derive from an inference of probable causation (not unambiguous causation but probable causation), which includes the possibility of purely coincidental consecutivity. The inference of probable causation, itself, derives from the concept of his own indeterminate volition. Probable causation implies nothing about the characters of the cause or the effect or even about their relationship. Probable causation derives only from indeterminate occurrences of the cause followed reliably by consecutive occurrences of the effect, and only suggests the probability of future consecutivity. When predictions based on probable causation achieve a particular level of reliability, one efficaciously forgets contrary possibilities and treats the relationship as unambiguously causal, not probably causal but definitively causal. The causal explanation loses its tentativity and becomes a belief. At that stage, the history of reliable predictions has identified a domain of circumstances in which predictions are expected to be reliable. In choosing one's own behavior, one has no practical alternative but to adopt the concept that one's behavior is unambiguously caused by one's volition. There is a very large practical domain within which one is confident that adoption of the personal belief will lead to value. But there is also a small separate domain (the limited domain of the scientist conducting brain surgery) in which the scientist efficaciously adopts the apparently contradictory concept that the physical phenomena within the subject's brain probably cause the subject's mental experiences.

There are several reasons why the scientist can simultaneously adopt both these beliefs of causation.

First, these beliefs may seem contradictory but are not. The scientist may reasonably conceive that different rules apply to his own experiences than to the subject's. The subject may not have experiences.

Second, the logic of causation only suggests probable consecutivity of cause and effect in the future and reflects nothing about the specific properties of the cause or the effect. Inferences of probable causation may be reasonable, even though the properties of the cause and effect may, in some other respect, suggest a contradiction.

Third, when comparing two apparently contradictory concepts from the elemental perspective, the problem is not to identify which is true or valid so that the other must be discarded. Rather, the problem is to define domains of efficacy for them both. Even if there is an apparent contradiction between the scientist's belief and the personal belief, it may be efficacious to adopt those mutually contradictory concepts within mutually exclusive domains. The idea that each concept has a domain within which its adoption is conceived to be efficacious permits adoption of all manner of apparently contradictory concepts within separate domains. Concepts that are contradictory in some respect do not give rise to a conflict (where one is obliged to choose one and not the other) if their domains are separate.

Within the domain of the scientist's practical medical or investigative purpose while he is manipulating the subject's brain, the practical understanding of causation of the subject's mental experiences by his physical brain phenomena (the scientist's belief) is efficacious, despite its limited profundity. That understanding has no depth and is not a scientific understanding, nor will it become a scientific understanding as described in Chapter Six. For the scientist's personal purpose of coping with practical life and within the separate domain of directing the behavior of his own body, his understanding of causation of his bodily behavior by his volition (his personal belief) is also efficacious. These are separate domains even though they are both adopted by the scientist at the same time during the course of the experiment. The domain of the personal belief concerns the relations between the scientist's experiences and his bodily behavior. The domain of the scientist's belief concerns the subject's experiences and the subject's brain phenomena. The domain of the personal belief is very large in the sense that there are countless decisions that the scientist will make in the course of his life where he efficaciously adopts his personal belief. However, the practical personal belief does not satisfy the scientific standard of understanding.

Scientific understanding derives from observations of scientists conducting experiments, and in order to conduct the experiments, scientists must individually adopt personal beliefs that their own indeterminate volitions cause the behavior of their bodies. The personal belief forms part of the conceptual substructure of scientific understanding.

The domain of efficacy of the principle of individual responsibility is very, very large. The separate domain of the concept that instantiation of physical brain phenomena cause mental experiences is very, very small. The area of overlap of these two domains (which is considered immediately below) is yet smaller by orders of magnitude. Even if the advance of science should significantly expand the domain in which it is efficacious to adopt the concept that instantiation of physical brain phenomena causes mental experiences, it is difficult to imagine how the very much larger practical domain of individual responsibility might be significantly reduced. The advance of brain science does not threaten the responsibility of individuals for their acts of volition. The practical domain in which it is efficacious to adopt the concept that volition causes bodily behavior will always be many orders of magnitude larger than the domains of concepts of physical causation of mental experiences.

The apparent contradiction suggested by examples where mental experiences cause physical phenomena and vice versa is largely resolved when one recognizes the separate domains within which the different causal explanations are efficaciously adopted. One can try to imagine a circumstance where the domains overlap, where the scientist assumes the roles of both experimenter and subject.

Imagine that the scientist manipulates his own physical brain to cause particular experiences of his own. What would the scientist/subject experience? First, in his role as scientist, he would experience the experiences that constitute the sequential volitions that he experienced when he acted only as scientist and directed the behavior of his body to do the manipulation of another subject's brain (experimenter-role experiences). Those volitions include the personal belief that his volition causes the bodily behavior that constitutes the manipulation. At the same time, he

would be adopting the scientist's belief that instantiating particular physical phenomena cause particular mental experiences. Even here, however,
the personal and the scientist's beliefs have separate domains so long
as the particular mental experiences that he is trying to cause are different from the mental experiences necessary to conduct the experiment.

Second, in his role as subject, he would experience a second category
of experiences: the experiences that he induced by the manipulation of
his brain (subject-role experiences). In this experiment, the experimenter and the subject are one person playing both roles, and, while it
may be helpful to understand his experiences by dividing them into
experimenter-role and subject-role categories, the scientist is only one
person and, within one unit of mentation this one person can experience only one concept of reality (stage 2) and only one concept of the
one behavior that is in his best interest to attempt (stage 4).

Suppose that the subject-role experiences (those intended to be induced
by the scientist) would be the experiences that constitute the volition to
do something other than conduct the experiment. The experiment
would seem to create two contradictory volitions: the experimenter-role
volition to conduct the experiment and the subject-role volition to do
something else. One can have only one volition at time and the experimenter-role volition cannot merge with the contradictory subject-role
volition into one coherent volition. There is no one behavior that can
do both. But these contradictory volitions would not be experienced at
the same time. The experimenter-role volition to instantiate the physical phenomena would be experienced in one unit of mentation, and
(assuming that volition was implemented in stage 5 of that unit of
mentation) the subject-role experiences would be experienced in the
next unit. The domains would still be separate.

No matter how one designs an experiment, contradictory concepts cannot
be forced into the same domain. The point of the thought experiment is
to prove neither that physical brain phenomena cause mental experiences, nor that mental experiences cause physical phenomena. From the
elemental perspective, both these concepts have full potential efficacy,

but to the extent that they contradict, their domains will be mutually exclusive. Contradictory concepts may be efficacious, but only within separate domains. The point of the experiment is to illustrate that both concepts have domains, and the result of any experiment designed to investigate any potential overlap of the domains will only serve to define the fine contours of those domains, not to identify a philosophical truth.

From the elemental perspective, both the scientist's belief and the personal belief serve as an efficacious basis on which to make predictions within particular domains. At times, one may face a practical problem to define the precise boundaries of those domains, but this difficulty is a practical, not a philosophical, problem. Elementalism recognizes numerous intellectual limitations (for example, the inability to conceive constituents of elemental experiences) and practical difficulties (for example, the inability to reconcile the wave/particle characteristics of quanta coherently). But a philosophical problem would be one in which the elemental principles themselves embody a contradiction. From the elemental perspective, the scientist's and the personal beliefs are not philosophically right or wrong. Rather, each concept is an elemental experience that was created to relate other experiences logically as a solution to a problem posed within a unit of mentation for the purpose of maximizing value. Seen thus, these apparently contradictory beliefs both fit coherently within the grand overall network of all concepts analyzable according to the elemental model of mentality. The only subject not analyzable according to the elemental model is elemental reality itself. From the elemental perspective, present experiences can be only experienced, not analyzed. Present experiences constitute the reality within which any analysis or recognition can occur. No conceptual system can serve to analyze or validate its own foundations. What one identifies as an analysis consists of present experiences purporting to analyze past experiences.

Compare the pragmatic concept of water with the scientific concept of an aggregate of H_2O molecules at a particular temperature and pressure. The domain of the scientific understanding is very small because there are far too many H_2O molecules in any quantity of water at the human scale for their individual interrelations to be managed. Scientists never-theless recognize that the scientific understanding is more profound than the pragmatic because the scientific (if only in principle) includes the pragmatic and could, in principle, substitute for the pragmatic wher-ever the pragmatic is efficacious — the scientific would be efficacious in other circumstances as well. Can one make a similar comparison, in terms of profundity only, between the scientist's belief and the personal belief? Does one include the other in some way? The scientific belief offers a theoretical way physically to induce any experience including the experiences that constitute volition and, consequently, bodily behavior. Seen this way, the scientific seems to include the personal. On the other hand, the scientific belief requires that the scientist, first, have a personal belief in order to conduct experiments to manipulate brains which he must do before he can create the scientific belief. Seen this way, the scientific belief seems to be a superstructure dependent entirely on the personal belief, and the scientific, therefore, could not completely displace the personal belief. I offer no resolution, but since the personal belief is philosophically essential to the scientific belief, my impression is that the personal is the more profound.

CHAPTER EIGHT

SUBSIDIARY
ISSUES

BEHAVIORAL SUPERFLUITY OF MENTAL EXPERIENCES

F ROM the practical, scientific perspective, each person is composed of physical elements, each person experiences his own private mental experiences, each person represents a separate mind/matter problem. The physical behavior of each person is determined by all the physical elements that make up the brain/body system and the surrounding physical elements with which those of the brain/body interrelate. The physical elements in brains interrelate there according to the same rules that apply to physical elements everywhere else. Causal exhaustivity implies that mental experiences play no part in the rules governing the behavior of physical elements anywhere else, nor is there reason to expect that brain tissue might be uniquely affected by non-physical causes such as magic spirits or subjective experiences. This suggests that mental experiences may be superfluous to the physical behavior of each individual. If mental experiences are superfluous to individual behavior, then mental experiences are superfluous to individual social (including reproductive) success that depends only on individual behavior, not on private experiences. A scientific description of the interrelations of the physical elements of which each individual is composed and with which each individual interrelates would describe each individual's physical behavior completely, whether or not there were private mental experiences accompanying that physical activity. From the practical, scientific perspective, this is true for each individual, and each individual represents a separate mind/matter problem. From the practical scientific perspective, there is no difference between oneself and anyone else in these respects.

From the elemental perspective, the view is quite different: there is a fundamental difference between oneself and everyone else. Elemental experiences (one's own mental experiences) are the elements from which everything is composed, including what one calls physical reality, which in turn includes one's own body and the bodies of other people. For elementalism, the bodies of other people do not experience private experiences of their own; they are themselves composites composed from one's own elemental experiences. Composites of experiences do not experience elemental experiences of their own: there is only one elemental level. In the elemental universe there are no experiences not one's own, no private experiences of other individuals to which one is not privy. One can fantasize experiences similar to one's own in other people, and the fantasy exists as a concept of one's own, but there are no experiences other than one's own. For elementalism, there is only one mind/matter problem: one's own.

One develops a concept of practical social reality with which one successfully predicts the behavior of other people by fantasizing what one would experience in their situations. That fantasy is part of the elemental substructure of the practical concept that other people experience their own experiences. In practice, it is much more facile to ignore the substructure — to relegate it to deep background. Thus, the concept that others have their own experiences becomes a belief. That belief exists as an experience of one's own. In practical circumstances, it is efficacious (for reasons of facility) to ignore the fantastic substructure of the concept that other individuals experience their own private experiences, but for philosophical reflection (where efficacy is measured only by profundity), the entire conceptual structure must be analyzed.

For elementalism, other people do not have their own experiences. What one calls "other people" is part of what one calls "physical reality." Other people have the characteristics of all other physical things, but all physical things exist as aggregates of one's own experiences. Consequently, it is not philosophically troubling that there might be a domain in which it is efficacious to understand the behavior of other people according to the same concepts that explain the rest of physical reality rather than by the fantasy that they have their own private experiences. It is not troubling that private mental experiences of other people might be superfluous to their behavior because, for elementalism, they do not have experiences. It is not philosophically troubling that a complete scientific understanding of the behavior of other people would not include any reference to private experiences of their own; it would be purely a description of physical elements interrelating according to the laws of physics, and that description would be complete.

One's own body (including its behavior and including the part of it called the "brain") is as amenable to a complete physical description as any other body. That description would include only relations between physical elements without reference to mental experiences. The physical understanding of the behavior of one's body would be quite different from one's own practical concept of personal responsibility, different from the concept that one's volition causes much of the important behavior of one's body. Both understandings would involve the behavior of the same body, but each would explain the behavior in terms of different causes. That each of the concepts identifies different causes does not imply that the two concepts contradict each other. One's own practical concept might be efficacious and, at the same time, a physical description might be complete. Both could be efficacious within their own domains and yet not contradictory. Even though the physical description would not include within it any reference to mental experiences, that physical description would exist only as an intellectual experience, which one could only understand within the context of mentation. The description would not include mental experiences as a part of the description, but the description would be included within the universe of experiences.

The comparison here is between one's personal belief and a scientific description of the behavior of one's body. This is a different comparison from that between the personal belief and the scientist's belief, considered in the previous chapter, concerning the subject of an experiment whose brain the scientist manipulated to cause experiences of the subject. That chapter illustrated how the personal belief and the scientist's belief have mutually exclusive domains. But the two concepts compared here, the personal belief and the scientific description of one's bodily behavior, which does not involve brain manipulation to cause experiences, would not necessarily have mutually exclusive domains. The two concepts compared here need not be mutually contradictory.

I cannot imagine a circumstance where a complete physical description of one's body would be a more efficacious means of understanding one's present volitional bodily behavior than one's personal belief. Imagine, however, that one has access to a computer that could fully describe one's physical constitution, and imagine the monitor of this computer can somehow display that complete description. One could look at the monitor just as one can look in a mirror. The image of the surface of one's body in a mirror reflects only physical phenomena, but one's interpretation of that image does not contradict one's concept that one's volition causes one's bodily behavior. The computer display would offer a complete description of one's physical constitution, and, like the image of one's body in a mirror, that description would make no reference to mental experiences. Neither would it contradict one's concept that one's volition causes the volitional behavior of one's body. Both descriptions would offer explanations of bodily behavior.

Were one to look at a monitor whose image reflected one's entire physical constitution, the image would give rise to physical phenomena corresponding to visual experiences, and those phenomena would then be registered on the monitor, which would in turn effect the visual physical phenomena, and so on. This feedback loop might seem like the familiar philosophical territory of infinite regress. One does not have the visual or intellectual capacity, however, to discern an infinite number of infinitesimal gradations, and therefore, the number of regressions would stop at some manageable number.

In whatever circumstances a complete physical description of one's present behavior might be efficacious, the concept that one's experiences are superfluous to one's bodily behavior also would be efficacious. The domain of such a concept must be very small, whereas the domain of personal responsibility always will be very large. The domains might overlap without contradiction. The possibility that a physical description of one's bodily behavior would be complete without reference to mental experiences does not contradict the practical model that one's volition causes one's volitional bodily behavior.

Assume, however, that there is some contradiction. Perhaps the complete physical description implies causally exhaustive determinacy and predictability that contradicts free will in such a way that the complete physical description is more profound (explains more) than does one's practical understanding of reality. Philosophy concerns only the profundity of concepts, not the size of their domains. If the complete physical description were more profound, then, philosophically, it would supplant one's practical understanding. Even so, the physical description would still stand on an elemental foundation. The physical description would still exist only as an intellectual experience, as part of the universe of present elemental experiences. Even if a complete physical description were to contradict and philosophically to supplant one's practical understanding, the physical description still would not contradict the elemental model of mentality.

THE HARD PROBLEM

I understand the term "hard problem" as that which a scientist has (from his practical perspective) to explain how subjective experience without physical manifestation might arise from physical brain phenomena. In this general form, the hard problem is the same problem that is addressed in Chapter Six. However, the hard problem is often expressed in terms of "what experiences are like." How can one know whether "what one's experiences are like for oneself" are the same as, or different from, "what another person's experiences (or a bat's) are like for him"? Are "what my experiences of 'red' are like for me" the same as, or different from, "what your experiences that you call 'red' are like for you"? To "be like" is synonymous with to "be similar to." It makes no sense to discuss what any particular thing "is like" except in terms of a comparison with something else to which the particular thing might be similar. For example, which of one's own experiences might "be like" the echo-locationary experiences that a bat experiences? What experience or combination of one's own elemental experiences might be similar to the echo-locationary experiences of a bat? Call this the "comparative" form of the hard problem. Whereas Chapter Six above addressed the general form of the hard problem, this chapter addresses only the comparative form.

From the elemental perspective, elemental experiences are not "like" anything, certainly not like anything else. An elemental experience itself is "what it is like." "What an experience is like" is nothing different from the experience itself. The comparative form of the hard problem is sufficiently stated without reference to what experiences are like: how can one know whether one's experiences are the same as another person's experiences?

There is a reason, however, that the hard problem is stated in terms of "what experiences are like." To state the hard problem in terms of "what experiences are like" suggests a difference between an experience itself and "what the experience is like." People who discuss the hard problem are mentally competent, practical individuals and naturally are very loath to contradict the basis of their mental competence: their fundamental practical beliefs. In any communication between philosophers (or anyone else) of abstract intellectual content, the underlying protocol of the communication includes the recognition by the communicator that the communicatee has the capacity to understand the communication, i.e., that the communicatee experiences the same types of elemental experiences as the communicator. To suggest that the communicatee does not experience experiences would contradict the protocol underlying the communication and might be insulting. The communicator recognizes that there is something unique about his own experiences (they are unique in that he experiences them and he doesn't experience any others; that uniqueness is the subject of the hard problem), but the communicator is in a dilemma because he can think of no way dispassionately to discuss that uniqueness without violating the protocol and being insulting. To solve this dilemma, the parties invent the diplomatic idea that there is a difference between an experience and "what the experience is like." With that invention, the communicators can both proceed without violating the protocol, and neither is insulted since each recognizes the other's full capacity to experience experiences and the other's mental competence. They can both agree that they each experience equivalent experiences, but neither knows "what those experiences are like" for the other. However, to acknowledge that one cannot know "what another person's experiences are like" (this is the definition of the comparative hard problem) is merely a polite way to acknowledge that one cannot know *anything* about another's experiences (not just "what they are like"). To say that one can know nothing about something includes that one cannot know whether it exists. If one cannot know whether something exists, then it can never have an effect on one and does not figure in one's universe. There's no point contemplating it. Posing the hard problem in terms of "what experiences are like" implies that private experiences of other people or bats do exist, and that it is merely "what those experiences are like" that cannot be known.

I have used the term "philosophical contemplation" throughout because contemplation is a solo effort that does not involve the participation of anyone else. Were anyone else involved, the potential for insult and the protocol of civilized communication would amount to an a priori bias making difficult the dispassionate consideration of the concept that other people do not have experiences. By using the term "contemplation," I hope to avoid the philosophically corrupting influence of potential insult. The consideration of elemental philosophical matters is necessarily solo contemplation. Even so, there is additional difficulty to recognize that the solo subject (oneself) does not have an independent elemental existence but is itself a composite of elements.

For many problems, the solution is not an answer in the form that the problem is stated. Rather, the solution is to recognize that the statement of the problem contains a fallacious premise. So it is with the comparative form of the hard problem. The fallacy in the premise of the hard problem is the idea that there are things in the universe other than one's own experiences, i.e., private experiences of other people.

From the elemental perspective, the sole constituents of the universe are one's experiences. Some of those experiences are concepts that organize external sensory experiences and constitute one's model of physical reality. Provided one recognizes that one's model of physical reality is merely an organization of one's external sensory experiences and does not refer to something that has an independent existence, one's model of physical reality has the potential to be philosophically coherent with its elemental substructure even though the hypothetical explanations of some physical phenomena contradict the hypothetical explanations of other physical phenomena — provided that the contradictory explanations have separate domains. Part of the model of physical reality consists of concepts of the physical bodies of oneself and other people. So far as those bodies have the characteristics of the rest of physical reality, the overall model of physical reality may be coherent. The model remains coherent if one associates one's experiences with the physical location of one's body, provided one continues to recognize that one's physical body is a composite composed from one's experiences and that the experiences are not constituted from the physical elements that make up one's body. (There is practical efficacy in the concept that experiences are physically constituted, but philosophically that concept introduces an incoherence into the model of physical reality. See Chapters Six and Seven.) The concept that other bodies are the physical location of "private experiences" is a fantasy deriving from the attribution to those bodies of the experiences that one experiences if one fantasizes oneself in their positions. That fantasy (which exists only as an intellectual experience of one's own) is efficacious in any social situation, and its importance cannot be overemphasized. The concept that other people have experiences, seen as a fantasy that exists within the universe composed from one's own experiences, is coherent with the grand elemental conceptual structure. But if the concept of other people's experiences is not recognized as a fantasy composed of one's experiences and, instead, if other people's experiences are treated as embodying their own philosophical elementality equivalent to one's own experiences, then the concept of other people's experiences is philosophically incoherent with the otherwise coherent model of physical reality. The fantasy of other people's experiences has practical efficacy, but the concept of other people's experiences with elemental existence equivalent to and independent from one's own experiences is a philosophical leap.

The answer to the hard problem is this: The statement of the hard problem contains a fallacious premise, a philosophical leap, i.e., that other people have private experiences. Everything that follows from that leap will also be fallacious, notwithstanding potential practical efficacy. Philosophically, it does not matter whether one decides that one's experiences are the same as, or different from, another person's because consideration of the problem in those terms itself involves a departure from philosophical rigor. One does not leap further from philosophical rigor by attributing particular characteristics to the experiences of other people when those experiences are not part of the universe. As a practical matter, it is crucial correctly to characterize the experiences of other people, but philosophically one is free to fantasize whatever one wants.

One reason it is hard to understand the essential nature of the experiences of other people is that it is hard to acknowledge that the basis of one's social competence is a fantasy. But before one can fantasize the private experiences of other people, one must first conceive the physical reality of other people. If it is hard to understand that the "experiences of other people" are constituted from one's elemental experiences, then it is even harder to recognize that even their "physical reality" is constituted from one's elemental experiences. Furthermore, if it is harder to recognize that what one calls "physical reality" is composed from one's

ELEMENTALISM AND THE MIND/MATTER PROBLEM

elemental experiences, then it is hardest to acknowledge that oneself is also composed from elemental experiences.

EVOLUTIONARY SUPERFLUITY OF MENTAL EXPERIENCES

If mental experiences are superfluous to individual success, then they are likewise superfluous to the evolutionary success of our species. The result of evolution is presumed to be the aggregate of characteristics that have historically assisted in successful replication of individuals. If mental experiences were superfluous to successful replication, why would mental experiences develop and persist within our species?

Some characteristics do not themselves contribute to successful replication but nevertheless persist because they are ancillary adjuncts to ones that do (spandrels). From the practical perspective, we consider our particular mental experiences to be the major characteristic of our species and not just an ancillary spandrel; therefore, it might be troubling if our major characteristic played no part in our success as a species.

Since evolution is the description of the history of particular physical things (all of the individual members of individual species, none of whom are oneself), it should not be troubling that there might be a small domain in which it is efficacious to understand that history as the behavior of constituent physical elements without reference to private mental experiences that any of those individuals might have had. The possibility of a domain within which a purely physical description of evolution might be efficacious for reasons of profundity does not contradict the possibility of a separate larger domain within which it might be efficacious for reasons of facility to understand evolution as a process involving the behavior of individuals caused by their private volitions. Call that more facile understanding a "fantastic description." The purely physical description would be more profound than the fantastic because the physical description would describe not just the development of living species but the larger set of all physical things.

Of course, the physical description of evolution, even though more profound than the fantastic description, leads to the bifurcation of knowledge into the sciences and the humanities unless one recognizes that both descriptions exist only as part of the larger, all-inclusive elemental universe. From the elemental perspective, the development of the universe began with one's earliest experiences, and current concepts of physical elements and evolution of living species are comparatively recent arrivals, with limited domains. Both the physical and the fantastic descriptions of evolution exist as concepts within the all-profound elemental organization of all experiences. Within that organization, those descriptions are neither true nor false. Rather, they are efficacious within domains defined by that organization.

One cannot conceive how mental experiences might be constituted from physical phenomena (Chapter Six, above). This conceptual limitation cannot be circumvented, just as one cannot conceive the square root of minus one within the real number system. Nevertheless, mathematicians created the imaginary number system, and, fortuitously, it has practical application. What follows is a description of an imaginary robot designed to have experiences that serve a function in its decisions.

Imagine a robot in which the brain-computer part is designed to imitate mentation. Its speed and memory are finite. The robot body has external and internal sensors that create information that is processed by programs within the computer to result in information analogous to external sensory and internal bodily experiences. The computer has programs analogous to each of the families of elemental experiences. Call these "elemental programs." The intellectual program has logics analogous to one's own (for example, it can infer probable causation). There are programs that relate the elemental programs to each other in a manner analogous to the mentation process. Call these "mentation programs."

Using these logics, the intellectual program identifies relationships between information produced by the other elemental programs, and these relationships are analogous to the simplest, least-compositive concepts whose original experiences are initiating experiences. The intellectual program stores relationships that it recognizes, and can recognize relationships between relationships — these would be analogous to composite concepts. Were such programs designed by a designer to mimic the designer's mental experiences, that designer would recognize the analogy between the programs and his own experiences, but to anyone else (except possibly for someone else who fortuitously recognized an analogy to his own mental experiences), the functioning of the computer would be understandable only as physical elements relating to one another according to the laws of physics. The physical activity alone does not suggest that the physical robotic system experiences private mental experiences. By the same reasoning, the physical activity of brains does not suggest that they have mental experiences either.

Physical elements behaving according to the laws of physics (such as colliding billiard balls or charged quanta interacting) imply or infer nothing in the nature of design or meaning. A complete understanding of brain physics would determine bodily behavior, but it would not, itself, suggest anything in the nature of the principles according to which (or the purpose for which) the functioning of the brain was designed. Reverse engineering (the inferring of the principles of the design of a system in terms of its purpose) is possible only because the reverse engineer can impute (from some source other than the system) a purpose to the design. Without a reverse engineer vicariously imputing purposeful design principles to a physical system, the behavior of the system is understandable in terms of physical elements relating to one another, but in no other terms. The behavior of a computer is understandable as the interrelation of its physical elements, but the dots and dashes (though entirely predictable) can imply no additional meaning (the meaning that the programmer intends) without the reverse engineer vicariously and creatively imputing a meaning from some source other than the physical elements. Were one able completely to reverse-engineer a brain, the physical activity would be understandable as physical activity, but it would not suggest anything of the principles of the design (such as elemental experiences or mentation) without the reverse engineer creatively imputing design principles analogous to his own mental experiences.

At any point in time within the computer/robot, the external and bodily sensors produce information that is processed by the external sensory and internal bodily programs, the result of which is information analogous to external sensory and internal bodily experiences. The intellectual program then processes that information. The result of the processing by the intellectual program is information analogous to the intellectual interpretation of internal bodily and external physical reality. That information is then processed by the emotional programs, and the result is information analogous to behavioral desires (and the other aspects of emotional experiences), which the intellectual program then processes into information analogous to a decision as to which output to activate. This information in turn is translated into some type of electrical signals controlling the motors that operate the body of the robot. All of this information processing is just mechanical physical activity, and the behavior of the robot is fully understandable as a system of physical elements without reference to mental experiences of the robot.

Assume that the computer/brain has an array of private monitors corresponding to the array described in Diagrammatic Representation, Chapter Two. The monitors cannot be observed externally. Assume that the computer is programmed to display an image on each monitor that reflects a brief description of the current status of the operation of each program. Mental experiences are analogous to the images on the monitor, and the sequence of these images would be analogous to the "stream of consciousness." The sequence of these images is organized in a manner analogous to the sequential stages within units of mentation during normal mentation as described in Chapter Two. The images on the monitors are analogous to mental experiences, even though no one watches the images. There is no homunculus — no person inside the robot watching its private monitors. So far in this thought experiment, the computer does not have a sensor watching its own monitors. The computer does not need to watch its monitors because it already knows what images are on the monitors, since it generated the information that led to the images. The images on the monitors result from the physical phenomena within the computer (not vice versa), and the computer can do the same computing that leads to the behavior of the robot whether the monitors are operating or not. The images on the *monitors, therefore, would seem to play no part in the behavior of the robot — the monitors would seem to have no function. The images are merely superfluous physical accompaniments to the other physical events in the computer (call this arrangement "superfluous accompaniment architecture"). A robot with private, superfluous accompanying monitors would seem to be able to behave as well as one without monitors, but the robot with monitors would be less efficacious because it would have to carry around the extra weight of the monitors and it would have to dedicate processing capacity to create the images on the monitors. If the analogy between such a computerized robot and a mentating individual is appropriate, the physical brain machinery dedicated to mental experience would seem to be an evolutionary disadvantage. Compared with a species with the same mentation but without subjective experience, a species with mental experience would seem to have the evolutionary disadvantage of a larger, slower brain with the same functional task. Is this reasoning correct? What benefit might a robot derive from private monitors without a sensor to monitor the monitors? Might there be benefit if the robot could monitor its monitors? Might there be another architecture in which the monitor images are not a superfluous accompaniment to the physical activity?*

First, imagine an architecture in which the monitor images are not a superfluous accompaniment to the physical activity but a part of it (call this "functional image architecture"). Imagine that the various programs are discretely compartmentalized so that the information produced by the elemental programs serves only to create brief status reports that appear on the monitors. Assume that this robot is equipped with a sensor to view its private monitors and that the information created by this sensor, rather than the information created by the elemental programs, is processed by the mentation program.

When the sensor "senses" the monitor images, the "sensing" occurs by means of the sensor creating some type of information (dots and dashes) that is analogous to the monitor images. In this robot, all of the monitor images, the sensor, the information created by the sensor, and the processing of that information are physical phenomena. However, for the purpose of this hypothetical exercise, imagine that the monitor images and the sensing of the monitors somehow give rise to experiences by some means that one cannot conceive.

In this architecture, the private monitor images become part of the physical activity that constitutes the information processing that leads to the behavior of the robot. Of course, if the status images on the monitors were as complete and reliable as the information produced by the elemental programs that leads to the status images, then the decisions and the behavior of the robot under the functional image architecture would be the same as under the superfluous accompaniment architecture. However, if the imaging mechanism introduces some character of its own, then decisions under the different architectures would differ, but any "character" of the functional image architecture properly could be characterized as imperfect transmission of information rather than as an advantage. At a minimum, the monitors and/or the sensor that senses the monitors must introduce some new information that figures in the mentation process; otherwise, it would contribute nothing distinctive to the behavior of the robot, even though it would be part of the physical functioning.

Second, if brain/mental experience is analogous to computer/monitor image, mental experiences serve the same function for humans that monitors do for computers: they serve for communication. For normal computers, the display on the monitor plays no function in solving the problems that the computer solves. The only significance of the monitor is that it can be observed by, and thus communicate with, the operator of the computer. For most computers, the purpose of the monitor is to communicate information to a human: the communicatee is a human, a different species than the communicator. For a computerized robot designed to mimic a human, however, the communicatee must be another member of the same species, that is, another computerized robot with the same functional characteristics as itself. The programming of the computer must accommodate both sending and receiving the same communications. The question then becomes: How can private monitors (even given functional image architecture) serve for communication when the monitors cannot be observed by the communicatee? How can mental experiences serve for communication when they are experienced purely subjectively?

The evolutionary importance of communication between members of our species cannot be overstated. However, not every aspect of the physical activity within a brain needs to be communicated. We are barely able to understand/articulate what we experience. How much more difficult would it be to understand the actual physical activity that must underlie mental experiences if brains are analogous to computers? Efficient design of monitor display requires that the information displayed on the monitor be the minimum necessary to be communicated for two reasons: (1) Too much information can easily overwhelm the communicatee and thus defeat the purpose of the monitor display, and (2) a monitor display requires a dedicated program that is largely extraneous to the problem solving that the computer would be doing without the monitor display — a monitor display program absorbs processing capacity and speed. If brain/mental experience is analogous to an efficient computer/monitor, one has the experiences that one has because they contain the minimum information necessary to be communicated to and from others of one's species. If so, experiences are an abbreviated, simplified metaphor (a brief status report) for the physical information processing occurring in the brain. The degree of simplification and the lack of experience relating to underlying processing that presumably occurs reflect efficiencies that, again presumably, have been efficacious for our species during its evolution.

Consider the behavior associated with instinctive outputs. Whenever concentration focuses on a specific feeling (when one experiences a feeling), specific instinctive behavior follows. This instinctive behavior is part of the vocabulary of the universal language of feelings contained in facial expressions, postures, tones of voice, laughing, crying, and so on. There is, of course, ambiguity in the interpretation of these forms of behavior (not least because they are most often accompanied by learned behavior). They have no intellectual component and occur without any learning of the behavior or any decision regarding behavior. Presumably, communication by means of the universal language of feelings (being devoid of intellectual content from the communicator) is the simplest communication and was the earliest to develop. It is important for one person to know how another feels, and the universal language of feelings is the vocabulary, the catalogue of behaviors, that signify one's feelings.

In this thought experiment, the robot has specific behaviors that accompany the specific monitor images that are analogous to feelings. How can the computer/robot communicate with other members of its species using these behaviors as symbols of particular private monitor images? If an engineer were designing such a species of computer/robot, the easiest design would include a program to recognize other members of the species and to recognize the particular symbolic behaviors in them. For example, individual lights on the forehead of the robot could symbolize the operation of elemental programs representing specific feelings. However, a human does not recognize anything ab initio. Ab initio, a human is a cognitive tabula rasa. Logic is a hard-wired capability, as is instinctive behavior, but no concepts exist without being intellectually created from experiences. For the computer/robot to mimic mentality in this thought experiment, it must start with a logical capability and with instinctive behaviors that follow its private monitor images, which are analogous to feelings, but any recognition must be learned. The computer/robot has the capability of recognizing the temporal correspondence between particular monitor images (corresponding to feelings) and its own particular behaviors. "Its own behaviors" is a metaphor for patterns that it would recognize between other monitor images analogous to external sensory and internal bodily experiences. The computer could learn the relation between its own private monitor images, its own body, and its own instinctive behaviors, and it could then recognize other bodies of its own species and behaviors of the other bodies similar to its own behaviors. It could then understand the behavior of others as accompanying their private images similar to its own private images. This holds equally for all the images on the private monitor (including those analogous to the most complex intellectual concepts), not merely the simplest feelings.

The images on the private monitor then serve as a basis for the robot to learn to understand what is significant about certain of its own behaviors in order to infer that same significance to other members of its species in terms of hypothetical private images of theirs. For such a robot to communicate with others of its species, it must first learn to understand its own internal states, or, rather, it could understand communications from another of its own species only to the extent that it had previously learned to understand its own internal states. It is difficult to imagine a computer that could recognize anything about itself and others of the same species without the necessity of the abbreviations or simplifications of its own physical functioning, simplifications that, in this thought experiment, are represented by simple monitor images. One function then of private monitor images is to represent a very simplified status report of the functioning of the different programs. This simplification is the new information that functional image architecture introduces. This simplification permits communication of much less information than the full status of the programs. Were it possible, and could it be understood, communication of the full status of the programs would require huge amounts of time just to convey the information. Simplified status reports allow communication with speed.

The easiest way for an engineer to design a communicating computer/robot species is to maximize the initial knowledge and minimize the learning that is necessary. From the evolutionary perspective, however, knowledge may quickly become an archaic burden. An initial tabula rasa *maximizes flexibility to learn and represents the ability to adapt to the different circumstances that evolution presents. A second function of private monitor images, properly designed, therefore, would be to provide an adaptive learning capability that is an evolutionary advantage over hard-wired knowledge.*

If the monitor images of the functional image architecture in this thought experiment are analogous to mental experiences, mental experiences provide the vocabulary and meaning according to which one can learn to understand oneself and thereby learn to understand and to communicate with others of one's species. The success of our species demonstrates that the vocabulary is efficacious.

Were this robot to contemplate the constitutional relation between the physical elements that constitute its computer and the images on its private monitors (its experiences), it would confront its own mind/matter problem. Its intellectual experiences would consist of logical relationships drawn between the brief status reports of the elemental programs: those brief status reports are the elements from which those relationships were com-

posed. The relationships are syntheses of those elements and therefore cannot disclose anything about the constitution of those elements. To the robot, the brief status reports are the elements from which all its knowledge is composed. The robot would be conceptually incapable of identifying constituents of its elements. Its elemental perspective would give rise to the same conceptual gap that prevents one from analyzing one's own elemental experiences into more elementary constituents.

Analogizing one's mentality to a computer, only the capacity to experience elemental experiences and capacity to draw logical relations between them are hard-wired. The elemental model of mentality is the operating system, and practical reality is the program one uses for normal, waking life. The mind/matter problem is the problem of trying to understand the hardware of a computer by using a program that is itself based on, and operates only through, that hardware and an operating system.

MORAL AND LEGAL RESPONSIBILITY

The principle of individual responsibility is basic to the Western legal and moral tradition that holds each person legally and morally responsible for his voluntary actions but not for actions taken under compulsion. If one's reasoning is determined by irresistible brain physics, the issue arises whether all one's actions result from irresistible compulsion, rendering this basic principle of Western legal and moral responsibility fallacious.

The practical concept of other individuals with physiques and mentalities similar to one's own is the basis of one's understanding of interactions between people that affect their feelings and therefore the values that they experience. Impractical concerns, as for example whether or not there is an "actual" physical reality or whether experiences are fundamentally physical, are not normally issues of justice or morality because justice and morality presume practical reality and are applicable only to a practical reality containing other people with their own experiences. Morality and legality define some of the principles that one recognizes as regulating interactions between people according to the value that those interactions create. Value is the elementary currency according to which one measures interactions between people.

Chapter Two of this book describes the emotion of shame as the elemental basis of morality, and anger, of justice. Chapter Three outlines the concepts of practical reality and what constitutes a system of justice and/or morality. Hatred is an elemental constituent of such a system. Following is a summary of those descriptions.

> *All feelings have value, not only the emotions of shame and anger. The value arising from any particular interaction between people derives from all the different feelings associated with that interaction. A complete description of the moral or legal significance of any interaction would include all the associated feelings. What follows is only the briefest description of the necessary feelings (shame, anger, hatred), but any complex situation involves other feelings that would have to be included in a complete analysis.*

The concept that evokes shame is "personal failure to achieve a goal," and the value of any experience of shame is bad. Where the personal failure is intended to, and does, cause harm to another person, the shame that one experiences (in this circumstance called "guilt" or "one's conscience") is the inherent marker of immorality. The term "harm" means simply "bad value." The term "immoral" is applied to one's own behavior that causes intended harm to another person where the behavior is conceived as a personal failure. Within any system of morality to which one subscribes, the "goal" that one continually tries to achieve is to behave according to a standard of civility. That standard of civility defines when harm (bad value) that one intentionally causes to another is either (1) improper and ought to give rise to one's shame/guilt or (2) permissible and about which one may be indifferent. Community standards of civility differ, and great debates concern the appropriate standards for any particular communal circumstance (political and moral philosophy). Even within a well-established, stable community, it is a great intellectual achievement for an individual to conceptualize prevailing standards and behave accordingly. But whatever the community's standards and whatever one's degree of success in conceptualizing them, one has the inherent capacity to experience shame when one fails to maintain whatever one conceives to be the proper behavioral standard and intentionally causes harm to another person. Whereas immorality is conduct identified by guilt (elemental shame in a particular circumstance), morality is any other conduct. One is morally free to do anything that is not immoral, just as no conduct is subject to criminal sanction unless specifically prohibited by criminal legislation. Morality does not have its own elemental basis separate from immorality, separate from one's capacity to experience shame.

> There are degrees of immorality deriving from the degree of harm caused, but there are no similar degrees of morality. Criminal punishments are intended to be proportionate to the degree of immorality, but there are no analogous degrees of reward for obeying the criminal law. There is no specific reward for not committing a crime. The law does not legislate how one should behave (one is free to do whatever one wants), provided that one does not commit an immorality by violating a criminal prohibition. In any social circumstance, the breach of a prevailing social standard gives rise to some type of sanction. Consequently, one maintains the social standard of civility not only because of the shame that one would suffer in the breach but also because of the sanctions that one would expect to suffer. Social standards of civility and social sanctions for a breach are part of a system of morality. But one often finds oneself in a circumstance where one might be able to avoid the social sanctions of an immoral act, where one can derive benefit by causing harm to an innocent person with impunity. In such a circumstance, the prospect of guilt is the only factor influencing one to maintain the social standard. To forgo the benefit of a crime, which one could commit with impunity, solely to avoid guilt is said to be "saintly" or "genuinely moral."

The generic behavioral desire associated with shame is to hide or withdraw in shame and thereby keep the failure secret.

One recognizes one's own immorality in the experience of one's shame after one intentionally causes harm to another person in breach of one's own civil standard, but one does not experience another person's shame. One considers another person's conduct immoral (shameful) if it breaches one's own standard and causes harm to someone else — where, if one fantasizes oneself behaving that way, the fantasy gives rise to one's shame. Other than this type of fantastic, vicarious experience of shame, however, one does not experience another person's immorality. When one identifies immorality in another person's intentional behavior, one experiences the emotion of hatred.

The concept that evokes hatred is evil. Evil is the intention in another person to cause harm to one. The generic behavioral desire associated with hatred is the desire to eliminate the evil. Where evil resides in a person who is otherwise of some value, the desire is to eliminate (exorcise) the evil through retribution. But where the evil has permeated a person and cannot be exorcised, the desire is to kill the evil person — the person whose intention is to do harm to one. It is the appropriate strategy to deal with an incorrigible natural enemy without whom the (one's) world would be better off. All immoralities that one recognizes in another person are evils, but not all evils are immoralities. For example, an enemy soldier's intention to do one harm may not be prohibited by one's social standard and therefore would not be immoral, but that intention would be evil and would justify killing the enemy soldier.

The concept that evokes anger is a disrespect: an abrupt intentional interference by the perpetrator with the victim's attempt to achieve a goal. The generic behavioral desire associated with anger is the desire to punish the perpetrator of the disrespect. The object of punishment is to "teach a lesson" that the disrespect was improper. The punishment is appropriate when it achieves compensation for the disrespect and an acknowledgement (apology) that the perpetrator has learned the lesson.

The moral and legal economics of any interaction between individuals involves all the feelings (experiences that have value) of all the individuals involved in the interaction. The complete moral or legal analysis of any particular interaction between individuals includes the values of all the experiences involved in the interaction and not only the three emotions described above. For example, the harm component of shame or hatred would include the bad value of any feelings that the victim experiences. Whatever other emotions are involved, shame and hatred are always factors in moral analysis, and anger in legal analysis. A basic understanding of morality and legality must recognize that any combination of feelings may be involved in any particular interaction, but that only shame, hatred, and anger are necessarily involved where morality and justice are in issue.

Within any system of moral and legal responsibility, the significance of shame, hatred, and anger is that they constitute the elemental basis for sanctions: death or retribution to eliminate or exorcise evil, punishment to exact compensation and an apology for disrespect. To the person experiencing a sanction, its essential significance is that it is bad.

Each unit of mentation gives rise to one decision how to behave. The decision is the intellectual interpretation of the best single behavior to implement the hierarchy of behavioral desires corresponding to the hierarchy of values of the emotions experienced within that unit of mentation, within the present. Included in the concept of present reality is the concept of potential futures that in turn depend on the behavior that one adopts in the interim. If the concept of potential futures includes the sanctions consequent on the commission of an immorality or an illegality, the emotions generated by that concept should, in the game-theory economics of choosing the best future for oneself, act as counter-indications to the behavior that leads to those sanctions. Of course, one is free to choose to do whatever one wants, but the basis of one's freedom will be the mechanical mentation process, which follows its own rigorous logic and may be physically based and predetermined in some way that one cannot conceive. The point is that part of that decision-making process includes consideration of the counter-indicative significance of the sanctions. Sanctions work to support a legal or moral system in which individuals choose their own behavior so long as the counter-indicative significance of the sanctions associated with particular ways of behaving is part of the process by which individuals within the system make decisions about their behavior.

From the perspective of the victim of an immorality or an injustice, to administer the sanction is the inherent desire associated with the elemental emotions that he experiences. From the perspective of the perpetrator of an immorality, the sanction will be included in future decisions. In this way, the sanction instructs the perpetrator about prevailing standards. Learning from sanctions/instructions is one way to develop one's conscience and "sense of justice." The result, provided that the standards are appropriate to the evolutionary circumstances of the society, is a stable, self-reinforcing social system of morality and justice.

The Western systems of moral and legal responsibility are not based on individual, unstructured, whimsical mental freedom. Rather, they are based on the counter-indicative significance of sanctions within the process by which individuals choose behavior. That is, our legal and moral systems are based on the perpetrator's ability to learn. There would be no point in sanctioning the perpetrator of an immorality or injustice if his intentions were "free" of any structural constraints so that his behavior could implement either what he wanted or did not want irrespective of what he knew to be the consequences. However, if mentality were different and sanctions were more effective than they are, if the counter-indicative significance of sanctions prevented one from choosing particular behavior instead of being merely one factor in one's decisions (i.e., if individuals were even less "free" than they are), holding individuals morally and legally responsible (subject to sanction) for their misdeeds would lead to a social system even more stable, but less adaptable, than our own. Perpetrators may not learn from sanctions (punishment may not be an efficacious deterrent to crime), but victims nevertheless experience an elemental desire to punish evil and injustice.

Even if a determinate physical basis of mentality were the ultimate constitutional cause of the rigorous logical mechanism of mentation, the ability to learn from punishment would still remain, and that is the basis of Western morality and legality.

The principle that one is not responsible for acts taken under compulsion is consistent with Western morality and justice so long as the compulsion is understood to refer to external compulsion (an irresistible physical constraint on one's physical behavior or a sanction imposed by an external source that is worse [badness of greater magnitude] than the social sanction and thus operating to prevent one from doing what one would otherwise want to do). Sanction serves the purpose of teaching a lesson not to commit the immorality or illegality in the future or, in the case of profound immoralities, of eliminating the evil altogether. For the person who already wanted not to commit the immorality or illegality and who would not have done so but for an external compulsion, retribution or punishment is unnecessary because there is no evil to be exorcised or lesson to be learned. Rather, the evil is in the compeller, to whom retribution or punishment is properly directed.

The Western basis of legal and moral responsibility does not contradict a physical or determinate basis of mentality.

CONCLUSION

Philosophy, which has neither foundations nor boundaries, and lacks primary ideas and first principles, is a sea of uncertainty and doubt, from which the metaphysician never drags himself out. So I have abandoned reason and consulted nature, that is, the inner feeling which directs my belief independently of reason.

JEAN-JACQUES ROUSSEAU

HISTORICAL periods are amenable to different interpretations, and neat characterizations of historical periods are gross simplifications. Nevertheless, to me, the Enlightenment symbolizes enthusiasm for the idea that everything is understandable by the rigorous application of reason, whereas the subsequent Romantic period symbolizes an enthusiasm for passion and the legitimization of intellectual relativism. Enlightenment enthusiasm derived from advances in the sciences, but the sciences fail unambiguously to explain mundane matters of morality, justice, taste, and so on (the humanities). This failure gave rise in the Romantic period to the rejection of rigorous reason as a means to understand humanistic matters and to the apparent bifurcation of knowledge into two discrete bodies of sciences and humanities ever since. The point of contact between these two discrete bodies, or rather the point where the bodies ought to contact, is the mind/matter problem. The current success of science has led to a present bias (an enthusiasm characteristic of the Enlightenment) that the mind/matter problem has a scientific solution whereby the mysterious principles of the organization of knowledge within the humanities will, as science advances, be understood with mathematical precision as physical phenomena.

The application of the elemental perspective to the mind/matter problem leads to a conclusion consistent with the Enlightenment notion that all understanding comes through reason but, nevertheless, contrary to the present scientific bias. Science can deal with the humanities only by means of a Copernican leap of faith. The Copernican idea that the earth was just an ordinary planet and not the center of the universe was a great astronomical advance, but to consider subjective experiences as just an ordinary manifestation of an independent physical reality does not clarify mind/matter issues the way the Copernican model clarified the understanding of the solar system. The idea that there is nothing special about one's own experiences, that they are made of the same physical constituents as everything else, is an unwarranted philosophical leap despite its honorable Copernican humility. On the contrary, such a Copernican leap in elemental matters leads directly to the bifurcation of knowledge into the humanities and the sciences. Despite the essential efficacy of such a leap in the practical domain, all leaps are contrary to the commitment to rigorous reason to which science and philosophy must adhere.

Rigorous reason requires one to recognize that self-evident elemental mental experiences are the elements (the starting points, the stuff) upon which reason operates, that reason itself (logicality) is a property of elemental experiences, and that what one identifies as "objective physical reality" has no independent elementary existence apart from the mental elements from which it is composed. There is no contradiction between the scientific perspective and the elemental perspective, provided that the latter is understood to underlie and include the former in the same way that quantum physics underlies and includes classical physics. From one's inescapable elemental perspective, the universe is constituted from one's elemental mental experiences, knowledge is unified according to principles intrinsic to the structure of mentality, the sciences and humanities relate *inter se* and *intra se* by the same continuous seamless logics, and the bifurcation seen at the practical level dissolves at the elemental level. The Enlightenment identification of reason as one's only tool to organize information is vindicated.

INDEX

in the circle, 57
decisions, 53–54
instinctive, 8, 37–38, 39, 56
learned, 36–38, 56, 171

pain, bad value of, 49
perception, as composite of
   elements, 9
personal belief
   and behavior of one's body, 188
   and scientific belief, 184
personal responsibility
   belief in, 178
   for one's bodily behavior, 170–76
   principle of, 169–70, 181
   and volition, 176
philosophy
   of elementalism, 69–73, 92
   organizing principles, xiv
   and profundity of concepts, 189
physical elements
   in brains, 185–86
   categories of, 115
   laws of physics, 187
   and mental experiences, 124
physical phenomena, 114–19
   and brain activity, 119, 156
   definitions of, 125–7
   elemental understanding of,
    147, 150
   explanation of, 150
   images on monitors, 197–98
   as mental experiences, 122–23,
    151–65
   scientific understanding of,
    146–47, 150
   and visual experiences, 188–89
physical phenomenon, explanation
   of, 150
physical reality
   model of, 192

of other people, 193–94
physical world
   as causally exhaustive system,
    116–17
   one's model of, 154
   types of order of, 117
physics, classical mechanics, xiii–xiv
pity, and resentment, 17–18
plurality, concept of, 27–28
possession, 16–17
practical concepts, 94–95
practical reality, 71
   conceptual islands of, 99, 109
   and elemental reality, 107–9
   internal, 96, 101–5
   and knowledge, 108
   and laws of physics, 100
   mental competence and, 96
   natural concept of, 86, 94–107
   and one's self, 102–3
   physical, 96, 97–101, 103–5
   pragmatic understandings of, 150
   social, 96, 105–7, 186
predictions
   pragmatic basis for, 148, 150
   reliable, 90–91
present experiences, validity of
   concepts and, 78
present reality, 48
   concept of, 45–48
   of mental experiences, 69–73
   period of mentation, 59
   and potential futures, 50, 105, 207
   undeniable, 73–75
pride, and shame, 13–14
prodrome, 23–24
profundity
   of concepts, 82–85
   criteria of, 92
proprioception, concentrational, 32
psychological analysis, 64–65

psychology
  introspective, 166
  organizing principles, xiii–xiv
pure concepts. *See* abstract concepts
pure reasoning, concept of, 125

quanta, wave/property properties
    of, 145, 183

reality
  concept of, 46
  philosophical, 73–75
  physical, 45
reality problem, 45–48
reasoning, 20–22
  abstract, 30–31
  See also pure reasoning
reflexes, instinctive, 38
resentment, and pity, 17–18
responsibility. *See* legal responsibility;
    moral responsibility; personal
    responsibility
retrieval, process of, 23
revulsion (disliking), and attraction
    (liking), 16–17
rhythmic experience, 9
road map, illustration of stage-depth
    dimensionality, 47–48
robot
  and feelings behavior, 201
  to imitate mentation, 195–97
  with private monitors, 198
  without experience, 170
Romantic period, 211

sanctions
  elemental basis for, 207–9
  and social standards, 205
sciences
  and elementalism, 115
  See also knowledge, bifurcation

of scientific method, 97
  buzzer example, 136
  concept of, 124–25
  testing of predictions, 88–89
scientific theories, 114–19
  physical world and, 99
sense, 20–21
sense of balance. *See* acceleratory
    experience
sense of rhythm. *See* rhythmic
    experience
sensory experiences, hierarchy of,
    42–44
sexual appetite, 50
shame, 106
  and morality, 204–7
  and pride, 13–14
social competence, fantasy-based, 193
social reality, and behavior of others,
    105–6, 186
social system, of morality and justice,
    106–7, 204–5
sorrow, and joy, 17
spatial dimensionality, of reality, 48
spiritual experience, 11
spontaneity, 62
stage-depth illusion, 46–48
storage, process of, 23
strategic behavioral desires, hierarchy
    of, 49, 51–53, 63
stream of consciousness, 32, 49, 59
  and the monitors, 57, 197–98
subjective experience
  universe of, 57
  without physical manifestation,
    189–94
substructure
  abandonment of, 95
  and decision-making speed, 102
  as distant background, 108–9
  elemental, 93–94, 95